BLACK+DECKER

The Complete Guide to

LANDSCAPE
PROJECTS

Updated 2nd Edition

Stonework, Plantings, Water Features, Carpentry, Fences

COOL
SPRINGS
PRESS
Home and Garden Experts™

MINNEAPOLIS, MINNESOTA

Quarto is the authority on a wide range of topics.

Quarto educates, entertains and enriches the lives of our readers—enthusiasts and lovers of hands-on living.

www.quartoknows.com

First published in 2015 by Cool Springs Press, an imprint of Quarto Publishing Group USA Inc., 400 First Avenue North, Suite 400, Minneapolis, MN 55401 USA. Telephone: (612) 344-8100 Fax: (612) 344-8692

quartoknows.com
Visit our blogs at quartoknows.com

Cool Springs Press titles are also available at discounts in bulk quantity for industrial or sales-promotional use. For details contact the Special Sales Manager at Quarto Publishing Group USA Inc., 400 First Avenue North, Suite 400, Minneapolis, MN 55401 USA.

10 9 8 7 6 5 4 3 2 1

ISBN: 978-1-59186-638-1

Library of Congress Cataloging-in-Publication Data

Complete guide to landscape projects : stonework, plantings, water features, carpentry, fences. -- 2nd edition.
      pages cm
  At head of title: Black & Decker.
  ISBN 978-1-59186-638-1 (pb)
  1. Landscape construction. I. Black & Decker Corporation (Towson, Md.) II. Title: Black & Decker complete guide to landscape projects. III. Title: Landscape projects.
  TH4961.C6542 2015
  712--dc23
                                                          2015020782

Acquiring Editor: Mark Johanson
Project Manager: Alyssa Bluhm
Art Director: Brad Springer
Layout: Danielle Smith-Boldt

Front cover image © SCOUT

Printed in China

The following projects are © SCOUT and are used with permission:
Stone Wall Solution (page 102)
Waterfall & Pond (page 190)
Backyard Fireplace (page 202)
Outdoor Brick Oven (page 214)

NOTICE TO READERS

Contents

The Complete Guide to
Landscape Projects

Contents (Cont.)

Introduction

*L*andscape is a fairly broad word that, quite frankly, most homeowners don't use very often. We don't throw *landscape barbecues* on summer holidays. We don't fire up the riding lawn tractor and *mow the landscape* on Saturday mornings. In fact, if you ask most homeowners to show you the landscape, they'll probably direct you down the road to the nature preserve or disappear inside to find their favorite coffee table book from the horticultural society. So why is this book, which is intended for homeowners who love DIY, called *Landscape Projects*? Why not *Backyard Projects* or *Yard & Garden Projects* or *Cool Things to Do with Your Lawn*?

The answer is largely one of convenience. *Yard* and *lawn* and *garden* are all terms we use routinely to refer to our surroundings, but no single one of them fully captures the totality of our outdoor living spaces. Landscapes include plantings, turf grass, old trees, and new shrubs. But they also include patios, fences, decks, and garden walls. Yours may feature a vegetable garden, statuary, a doghouse or two, or even a couple of old Fords on blocks. In short, if it is part of the visual environment outside the doors and windows of your home, it's part of your landscape. And, in practical terms, this means that your goal of creating an awesome yard and garden is truly a matter of good landscaping.

In *Complete Guide to Landscape Projects* you'll find a wealth of projects that draw from just about every imaginable yard and garden element you can think of (with the possible exception of old Fords on blocks). Border and accent plantings, lawn care, building patios and pathways, creating arbors, sunscreens, and windscreens are all covered. So are some more unusual projects, such as making fire pits or wood-fired ovens. Along with the clear step-by-step instructions and photos you'll find for these and dozens of other projects, you'll also get just the right guidance you need to make decisions about which projects make sense for you. The result will be an outdoor living space that meets the practical needs of your family and looks exactly as wonderful as you'd like it to. And who knows—with some planning and careful work, you might be so pleased with the outcome that you really do invite your friends to stop over for a little landscape picnic.

Landscape Design

A home landscape is an outdoor living area that is developed element by element. It is a space that should be as well designed as any room in your house. As such, the act of landscaping your yard is to purposefully create your own environment, and often the key to this is to select a theme that follows certain principles. The theme can be wild or formal, subtle or bold. It isn't critical that you follow your themes dogmatically, but from a design viewpoint you'll be glad you chose one.

In this chapter:
- Design Principles
- Landscaping Styles
- Landscaping by Yard Size

Design Principles

The principles of landscape design center around five basic elements: line, form, mass, texture, and color. The first three are the backbone. The last two are the skin and clothes that add visual richness and depth. Like everything else in a landscape design, lines should be intentional; curving lines are less formal, and guide the eye, providing a sense of motion and action. Straight lines and angles are a more formal approach. They are a great way to succinctly organize the landscape or replicate lines in the home's architecture or natural lines in the topography.

A mix of plant shapes, heights, and forms adds visual interest to any landscape. Most often, you'll use natural shapes to complement or contrast one another. You can, however, use repetitive plantings to create a pleasing rhythm within the landscape. Texture and color should be threads you run through the design, deliberately placed to complement or contrast other colors or textures.

That all may sound a bit fancy and academic, but it's not. It boils down to this—you build a successful landscape one piece at a time. Your theme guides your decisions, including path style, plants, surfaces, and all the other choices you make for the landscape. Theme even determines the best accents to finish your design—from water features to statuary, structures such as arbors and gates, and ornaments such as gazing balls or sundials. You'll see a few of these principles and ideas shown clearly on the following few pages.

Be up front. It's easy to forget the front yard when planning your landscape, but that's a mistake. The varied beds bracketing the front door of this house feature a profusion of flowers and shrubs. The planting is composed so that the mass increases closer to the house. This guides the eye up from the lawn, to the structure of the house, and provides a lovely, soft visual transition from the flat to the vertical.

Add night-lights. The landscape at night can be every bit as much a draw as it is during the day. Proper lighting is key, both for safety and to illuminate the charm of your design. The pool in this yard is incredibly alluring lit from within, while the fire pit is a fascinating focal point that fairly screams, "Sit and relax." Notice the open-grid design of the outdoor floor—it's a great treatment to blur the distinction between plant life and hardscape.

Make your fences fancy. Fences can be far more than simple privacy barriers. You can use fencing to partition off interior areas, as a way to create small, intimate areas within the larger landscape plan. You can also use fencing as it is in this yard, as a design element in and of itself. The simple, repetitive vertical lines of this fence create a continuity that ties together different areas in a rambling landscape. Think carefully about the style of any fence you build—it may be the perfect opportunity to accent your landscape.

Divide your space. Creating separate outdoor "rooms" is a wonderful technique for designing around a large open expanse, such as a lawn. Here, a hedge and trellis arbor offer a visual boundary that creates a sense of mystery of what lies on the other side. The best landscape designs draw a visitor through the landscape, and that's exactly what's happening here. The homeowner has used the open area of the lawn to frame an interesting focal point—a wheelbarrow planter.

Double-down on romance. This is the traditional tiered "pineapple" fountain that suits many different styles of landscape or garden. The wide basin makes this a good choice for a bird garden because it doubles as a birdbath. The look is not ideal for informal gardens such as a country or cottage style, but it fits right in almost everywhere else. One of the great things about fountains like these is that you can use them as hidden-away surprise visuals, or as focal points in their own right, placed in the middle of a lawn, garden bed, or courtyard.

Introduce a water element. Water features are some of the most fascinating landscape elements. The koi pond in this large, wild landscape is accented with classic Eastern statuary. It's an informal, stylish look that is perfectly suited to the naturalistic surroundings, and livestock always bring color and fun into your landscape.

Mix materials to build visual interest. Effective, livable landscaping often entails creating different areas—different outdoor rooms—for different purposes. One side of this large yard has been dedicated to a sitting area defined by an open-spaced, square-cut stone patio with pebble infill. Bordered by groundcover and ornamental grasses, this area is as close to zero maintenance as you can get, and is also a drought-tolerant design.

Direct traffic. Use arbors, pergolas, archways, or gates as invitations, leading people where you want them to go in the landscape. Wood is an obvious choice for these types of structures because the material blends in well with the plant life in a lush landscape. A simple vine has been trained on this pergola with trellis side panels, softening the lines of the structure and further melding it into the surrounding landscape.

Try terracing. Slopes can be a big challenge for the home landscaper. There are lots of ways to deal with a slope, but one of the best and longest lasting techniques is to terrace the slope. This front yard features stacked timber retaining walls to create terraces filled with evergreens. It's a well-defined, easy solution that could successfully be applied to many different sloped sites. The solution is also fairly inexpensive—never a bad thing in a landscape design.

Freeform is fun. There are an amazing variety of pathway styles to choose from for your landscape. The steppingstones used in this setting are a simple-to-install option that can be arranged to accommodate just about any layout, such as following the shape of the lawn here. Steppingstones are excellent when used in or across an expanse of lawn, because mowing over them is a cinch. The look is informal, though, and you should be sure that it matches the design style you're trying to set.

Make room for art. Landscape sculpture can be the perfect way to put your fingertips on a design. Sculpture should be carefully chosen not only to suit the style of your landscape, but also to ensure that it survives the elements and ages well. A single sculpture is often more effective than a group of scattered collection throughout a garden or landscape. The abstract metal piece here perfectly complements the informal bed of trees and ornamental grasses in which it's placed. It will fit in just as well as it ages and acquires a lovely patina of rust.

Create an outdoor floor. Hardscaping—the use of hard surfaces in landscaping—offers great potential to get creative. Not only can you choose from a wealth of paving styles and materials, you can mix and match for dynamic effect. This mortar-set includes a formal linear field of bricks in various sizes and shapes, a thin border of flat black sliced pebbles, and an outer border of small, irregular stone pieces. It's enough to steal attention from any garden scene.

Landscaping Styles

Some yards are blank canvasses waiting to be painted. Your house may be a basic structure that doesn't urge you in any particular design direction, and the local plant life and terrain may not be particularly distinctive. In this case, the door is wide open for you to choose a landscape style that reflects your tastes, suits the layout of your yard, and nurtures the way you want to live in your outdoor room.

In other cases, the local environment and surroundings may provide very strong indicators of an appropriate landscape style. You'd be wise to listen to these cues. For instance, if your home is located in a desert region of a southwestern state, you'll probably want to develop your landscape design around certain plants and features common to the area, including succulents, water-conserving hardscape and groundcovers, and shade structures. A cottage garden would simply not fit and would always look like a sore thumb—just as a desert landscape would look wrong attached to a New England home.

The location of your home may allow for multiple design possibilities. A coastal home that isn't on the water, for example, could look great with a sand-strewn seaside landscape, a Mediterranean villa look, a cottage garden style, or even a formal design.

Start by looking at plants and outdoor structures in your area. Look beyond other yards to parks and botanical gardens that often present many different styles of landscaping. When you've narrowed in on a sense of the style that most appeals to you and would be most appropriate for your home and yard, begin refining your ideas by checking out the images on the following pages.

Echo your environment. It is often best if the landscape style takes its cues from the surrounding geography and climate. This is especially true when the environment and terrain are distinctive as with a seaside home, or the high chaparral shown here. The design of this large yard takes advantage of the bordering wide-open plain and mountain views by leaving the property undefined by a fence or row of trees. The native terrain is allowed to blend into the yard, and along with terraced patios, native plants are used sparsely, in keeping with the practical realities of the drought-prone region. An antique horse-drawn wagon is used as yard sculpture to reinforce the open-plains feel of the yard.

Landscaping Style: Modern Scenic

Repeat. Repeat. The trim, straight lines and spare aesthetic of a modern home begs for the same treatment in its landscape. The designer of this front yard has obliged, using simple, repetitive plantings featuring regimented rows of spiky foliage plants with plenty of space left between the plants. The beds are formed of the same geometric shapes that dominate the walkway and the house itself. The modern look has a bonus feature of a water-conserving, low-maintenance landscape.

Less may be more. Modern architecture is all about linear perspective and minimal ornamentation. Marrying a landscape to a modern house can be challenging, but not if you throw out the conventional wisdom of what a landscape should be. Here, a curving bed provides a modicum of visual relief from the hard lines that define both yard and house. The bed is planted with drought-tolerant, hot-weather species that require little in the way of upkeep. A lawn of hot-climate grass will go brown when dormant in the hottest part of the summer, but cut short it will still have a clean, sharp look in keeping with the rest of the design. When it comes to modern-style landscapes, less is often more.

Landscaping Style: Wooded Retreat

Show off your shade. Hardscaping such as the patio and garden wall shown here is the ideal way to define social and recreational areas within a wooded yard. The trees are left standing and undisturbed, and the use of natural stone fits right into the surroundings. Shade-loving annuals are excellent choices to bring seasonal color into the dappled landscape.

Keep it natural. Landscaping a wooded yard sometimes means bending to the will of the environment. The trick in working with a wooded landscape design is to balance the wholly natural appeal of a copse of trees with the variation the eye expects in a designed landscape.

Landscaping Style: The Formal Garden

Combine classic patterns. Distinctive architecture often sets a tone that the landscape can follow. Stone walls offer a stately look that is complemented by an entryway and side yard paved with a sophisticated brick pattern. A simple fence with latticework top panel and carriage lights provides a fitting boundary, while beds lined with trimmed ball-shaped shrubs and a three-tier fountain add a dignified polish to this design.

Prune a shrub or tree to add formality. Formal landscapes are defined by particular elements. Repetitive features such as the planters in this yard—and cultivated shapes like the topiary that occupy those planters—are both strong indicators of formal landscape style. Straight lines are another, established here in the weathered decking. If you're after a formal aesthetic, consider features such as these to define the look.

Landscaping Style: Magical Cottage Garden

You can't go wrong with roses. Cottage gardens are all about tumbles of flowering plants cascading across the landscape—especially roses. It's a joyously untidy, unconstrained look that seems haphazard and overgrown. In reality, cottage gardens require a good amount of maintenance to keep all the blooming plants healthy. You may fall in love with the romantic look, but unless you have a green thumb, think twice about trying to replicate this style in your own yard.

Train your plants well. A cottage-garden landscape style is best suited to small yards, and buildings that reinforce the style, such as Victorians, stone buildings, and of course, cottages. Training climbing plants—both roses and blooming vines—is a key part of the look. Lawn surfaces should be kept to a minimum and bordered by sprawling plants and blooming shrubs.

Landscaping Style: Grass-Covered Outdoor Room

Think theatrically. A big expanse of lawn is like a stage on which you can compose elements. Beds, trees, and other features can be unified into a coherent landscape design by wrapping lawn around them or vice versa. It's the thread that holds the look together. A peninsula patio such as the one in this yard becomes a platform for the audience—a place to not only unwind, but to enjoy the interplay of elements amid a sea of green.

Curved borders soften lines. The front yard lawn is a traditional landscaping element for the American home. But there's simply no need or excuse to settle for a boring green rectangle unaccompanied by any other signs of life. As this image clearly demonstrates, a variety of plantings creates a unique interplay between the solid green, flat surface and a mixture of plant colors and shapes. This front yard incorporates small trees, a trio of tall arbor vitae standing like guardians before the house, and a beautiful shrub bed with a scattering of mixed colors. Trees in containers add even more of an interest to the lawn's smooth, unvarying surface.

Landscaping Style: Zen Scene

Seek tranquility. Designers of Japanese gardens create drama from natural forms in the landscape. Typical of the style, slab steps seem to float up out of the earth in this garden, and a small evergreen has been manicured into tree form with cloud-shaped greenery. The idea behind each element is subtlety and restraint and a truly organic feel, as if nature itself had decided to lay a path or trim a tree.

Get centered. Decorative sculptures are often a part of Japanese-style landscapes. The design rarely incorporates more than one, and the sculpture is usually a culturally significant representation. This mini pagoda sculpture is typical, although seated Buddha sculptures are frequently used as well. The sculpture is usually nested among dense plantings and less often used as a centerpiece for a raked stone or sand bed.

Landscaping Style: The Country Retreat

Choose rustic furnishings. A pole arbor and matching bench provide a restful retreat in the middle of a foliage-dense country-style setting. Structures like arbors, trellises, planters, and fences are great ways to announce a style amid plantings that could cross over between several different looks. This structure with its overhead vine exclaims "country" through and through.

Capture chaos. Detailed screens, a pergola, and decking bring order to this landscape where the plants do not. They climb through fences and up posts, and create an irregular border. This is a great way to use contrast to your advantage—attractive, ornate, and orderly structures offset by unruly plantings to provide stunning surroundings.

Landscaping by Yard Size

Yard size affects landscape design in several ways. A large tree or significant water feature such as a reflecting pool may simply overwhelm a smaller yard. The styles you can choose will also be affected by yard size.

A small yard looks best when it incorporates one or two focal features, supported with plantings and surrounding background elements. Look for space-appropriate versions of popular structures and fixtures. Instead of a large centerpiece fountain, a wall fountain may be more in keeping with your yard size.

A medium-size yard has more possibilities. Some are given over to swimming pools, with the surrounding landscape design and plantings serving to make the pool look as natural as possible. A medium-size yard also allows you more flexibility in creating landscape mystery—a pathway winding out of sight into some concealed "secret garden" or restful refuge where you can hide away for a few contemplative moments.

A large yard is brimming with design potential. Large landscapes are often designed with sweeping open vistas serving the same role as empty "negative" space does in painting—to give rhythm and pacing to the overall design. Whether these spaces are hardscaped or grass, they usually entail less maintenance than a full-blown garden. Large yards also present the chance to include several different and distinct areas, such as a rose garden, lawn for recreation, and a pond. Use a pathway to unify disparate areas.

No matter how big your yard is, never let the size make you give up on good landscape design. Use a little creativity and the ideas shown here to find a beautiful solution for your yard, no matter what size it is.

Celebrate diversity.
Just because a yard is small doesn't mean it can't be diverse. And just because it's a front yard doesn't mean it has to follow some stereotypical formula for a lawn, spread out in front of foundation plantings. The designer of this front yard added a wedge-shaped bed with containers and a variety of plants. The shape itself adds a lot of visual interest, while a stone wall in front of the house creates the perception of visual depth.

Landscape Size: Small

Pack it in. Small-yard landscaping is all about maximizing potential. This eclectic design fits a lot into a tiny space. The centerpiece is a decorative brick seating circle with a path featuring bricks laid in a different direction. The design includes two shaped shrubs, a lovely detailed gate and fence, perennials and shade-loving groundcovers, and even a tomato plant in the middle of the front bed. The design leaves no lack of visual interest no matter where you're looking.

Build upward. Pergolas are wonderful structures for all yards, but they are an especially handy option if you're designing a small or medium-size landscape. Pergola designs are usually scalable, so that they can be altered to suit available dimensions. They clearly define a central area in the landscape (usually used for relaxation, socializing or both). They not only shade that area, allowing pleasantly mottled sunlight to come through, they can also support all manner of climbing plants—allowing you to go vertical with your garden greenery where space is at a premium.

Landscape Size: Medium

Divide but unify. You can make a medium-size landscape seem more expansive by breaking it into irregular shapes—something the eye always finds intriguing. The thread that holds this yard design together is a broad strip of brick edging. A long flower garden creates a stunning visual point of separation between the house and lush lawn surface.

Get a little negative. "Empty" space, like the arc of grass in this landscape, is an important element in medium landscapes. Not only is a space like this adaptable to many different activities, from cloud-gazing to a game of tag, it also serves the same role as negative or white space does in art; it is a visual pause that provides perspective for the more decorative elements of the raised beds and shrub border in the distance, and small plantings around the patio in the foreground.

Landscape Size: Large

Before

Turn a negative into a positive. A large, steep yard may seem like a difficult site on which to design a compelling landscape. A little creative landscaping and some lumberjacking, however, can bring a slope to life. This home stands atop a small hill and the grass slope that ran down to a viewing deck below was hardly an inspired visual. The designer used the slope as a canvas on which to place an amazing assortment of shrubs, trees, and flowering plants. Looking up, the slope is viewed almost as a vertical surface, giving the plantings maximum exposure and visibility. A broad stone staircase and landings look less intimidating surrounded by plantings.

After

Greenscapes & Gardens

Typically, yard renovation begins with taking a hard look at what you have in your yard and then clearing away the old to make way for the new. To that end, we walk you through clearing land, including the basics on how to remove the nuisance trees, invasive plants, and thorny brush that stand in the way.

Sometimes, clearing amounts to one tall task: taking down a tree. Perhaps removing the tree will open up a sightline and allow sunlight to brighten a gloomy corner of your yard. If the job qualifies as DIY, we show you how to fell a tree correctly. If your trees and shrubs just need judicious pruning to restore their ornamental shape, we'll show you how to do that too.

Once the subtraction is complete in your yard, it's time for addition. Planting trees is rewarding and benefits your property by providing shade, increasing property value and curb appeal, and blocking wind. You'll learn how to plant a balled-and-burlapped tree and how to create a windbreak.

Finally, we explain how to plant and care for annuals and perennials. You'll find out how to create landscaping and garden beds, how to use edging, and more. And to help you conserve water, we show you how to practice waterwise gardening.

In this chapter:

Pruners	Landscape fabric (optional)
Loppers	Safety glasses
Bow saw	Gloves
Weed cutter	Long sleeves and pants
Nonselective herbicide (optional)	

Clearing Brush

Nuisance trees, invasive plants, and thorny groundcovers latch on to your land and form a vegetative barrier, greatly limiting the usefulness of a space. Before you can even think of the patio plan or garden plot you wish to place in that space, you'll need to clear the way. If the area is a sea of thorny brush or entirely wooded, you'll probably want to hire an excavator, logger, or someone with heavy-duty bulldozing equipment to manage the job. But on suburban plots, brush can usually be cleared without the need for major machinery.

Dress for protection when taking on a brush-clearing job. You never know what mysteries and challenges reside on your property behind the masses of branches and bramble. Wear boots, long pants, gloves, long sleeves, and eye protection. Follow a logical workflow when clearing brush—generally, clean out the tripping hazards first so you can access the bigger targets more safely.

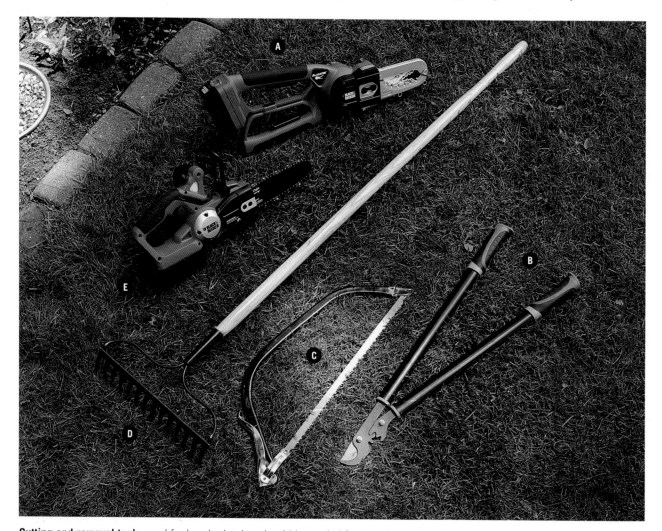

Cutting and removal tools used for brush clearing should be scaled for the job you're asking them to do. Simple hand tools can handle much of the work, but for bigger jobs having the right power tools is a tremendous worksaver. Tools shown here include: electric lopper (cordless) (A); loppers (B); bow saw (C); garden (bow) rake (D); chainsaw (cordless) (E).

How to Clear Brush

Begin by using a tree pruner to cut woody brush that has a diameter of less than 1½". Cut the brush and/or small trees as close to the ground as possible, dragging brush out of the way and into a pile as you clear.

Next, clear out larger plants—brush and trees with a diameter of about 1½" to 3½". Use a bow saw or chain saw to cut through the growth, and place the debris in a pile. Trees larger than 4" diameter should be left to grow or removed under the supervision of a professional.

Use a heavy-duty string trimmer or a swing-blade style weed cutter to cut tangled shoots, weeds, and remaining underbrush from the area.

Clear the cut debris and dispose of it immediately. Curbside pickup of yardwaste usually requires that sticks or branches be tied up into bundles no more than 3 ft. long. If you plan to install a hardscape surface, make sure the brush does not grow back by using a nonselective herbicide to kill off remaining shoots or laying landscape fabric.

Tree Removal

Removing trees is often a necessary part of shaping a landscape. Diseased or dead trees need to be removed before they become a nuisance and to maintain the appearance of your landscape. Or, you may simply need to clear the area for any of a variety of reasons, including making a construction site, allowing sunshine to a planting bed, or opening up a sightline.

If you need to remove a mature tree from your yard, the best option is to have a licensed tree contractor cut it down and remove the debris. If you are ambitious and careful, small trees with a trunk diameter of less than 6 inches can present an opportunity for DIY treecutting. The first step in removing a tree is determining where you want it to fall. This area is called the felling path; you'll also need to plan for two retreat paths. Retreat paths allow you to avoid a tree falling in the wrong direction. To guide the tree along a felling path, a series of cuts are made in the trunk. The first cut, called a notch, is made by removing a triangle-shaped section on the side of the tree facing the felling path. A felling cut is then made on the opposite side, forming a wide hinge that guides the fall of the tree.

Always follow manufacturer's safety precautions when operating a chainsaw. The following sequence outlines the steps professionals use to fell a tree and cut it into sections. Always wear protective clothing, including gloves, hardhat, safety glasses, and hearing protection when felling or trimming trees. And make certain no children or pets are in the area.

TOOLS & MATERIALS

Chainsaw	Ear protection
Hardhat	Wedge
Safety glasses	Hand maul

Hinge

Notch

Felling cut

How to Fell a Tree

Remove limbs below head level. Start at the bottom of the branch, making a shallow up-cut. Then cut down from the top until the branch falls.

NOTE: Hire a tree service to cut down and remove trees with a trunk diameter of more than 6".

Use a chain saw to make a notch cut one-third of the way through the tree, approximately at waist level. Do not cut to the center of the trunk. Make a straight felling cut about 2" above the base of the notch cut, on the opposite side of the trunk. Leave a 3"-thick "hinge" at the center.

Drive a wedge into the felling cut. Push the tree toward the felling path to start its fall, and move into a retreat path to avoid possible injury.

Standing on the opposite side of the trunk from the branch, remove each branch by cutting from the top of the saw, until the branch separates from the tree. Adopt a balanced stance, grasp the handles firmly with both hands, and be cautious with the saw.

To cut the trunk into sections, cut down two-thirds of the way and roll the trunk over. Finish the cut from the top, cutting down until the section breaks away.

Pruning Trees

Regular pruning of trees and shrubs not only keeps the plants looking neat and tidy, it makes them healthier.

Pruning trees and shrubs can inspire new growth and prolong the life of the plant. It may surprise you that the entire plant benefits when you remove select portions. Regular pruning also discourages disease and improves the plant's overall appearance.

Timing and technique when pruning will, quite literally, mold the future of the shrub or tree. The trick to properly pruning trees and shrubs is to remember that less is more. Instances that warrant pruning include: pinching off the ends of plants (to maintain a bushy look); restoring an ornamental's shape with clean-up cuts; and removing rubbing tree branches, where abrasion is an open wound for disease to enter.

Light, corrective pruning means removing less than 10 percent of the tree or shrub canopy. This can be performed at any time during the year. However, when making more severe cuts, such as heading back, thinning, or rejuvenating, prune when plants are under the least amount of stress. That way, trees and shrubs will have time to heal successfully before the flowering and growing season. The best time to perform heavy pruning/trimming on most woody plants, flower trees, and shrubs is during late winter and early spring.

SHRUB PRUNING

Use a combination of these pruning methods to control shrub growth.

Pinching: The terminal of the shoot is the tip of the stem (green portion before it becomes woody). When you remove the terminal, the bud is lost, allowing lateral buds to grow. Pinching reduces the length of a shoot and promotes side (filler) growth. Pinch off especially long shoots from inside the shrub canopy.

Heading back: Increase the density of a shrub by cutting terminal shoots back to a healthy branch or bud. Cut inward or outward growing shoots to manipulate the shape. Choose your growth direction, then remove

buds accordingly. The top bud should be located on the side of the branch that faces the direction you want it to grow. For example, an inward-facing bud will develop into a branch that reaches into the canopy. If you allow two opposite-facing buds to grow, the result is a weak, Y-shaped branch.

Thinning: This involves cutting branches off the parent stem, so target the oldest, tallest stems first. (You'll need to reach into the shrub canopy to accomplish this successfully.) Prune branches that are one-third the diameter of the parent stem. To visualize where to cut, imagine the Y junction, where a lateral branch meets the parent stem. Practice moderation when thinning.

Rejuvenating: Remove the oldest branches by leaving little but a stub near the ground. Young branches can also be cut back, as well as thin stems.

Shearing: Swipe a hedge trimmer over the top of a shrub to remove the terminal of most shoots; this will give you a formal topiary look. Shear throughout the summer to maintain the shape. Keep in mind, shearing is more aesthetic than beneficial: it forces growth on the exterior of the plant, which blocks light and oxygen from the center. You're left with a shell of a shrub—leaves on the outside, naked branches on the inside.

HEDGE TRIMMERS

An electric or gas-powered hedge trimmer isn't just easier to use, it offers much greater control than pruning shears for shaping hedges during the pruning process.

TREE PRUNING

Always prune tree branches by cutting just outside the tree collar. You'll notice a circular closure around the wound as the tree begins to heal.

Thinning: These cuts reduce the tree canopy and allow wind to pass through branches. Thinning is a safety measure if you are concerned that a storm will damage a tree and surrounding property. Remove dead, broken, weak, and diseased branches. Cut them back to their point of origin or to laterals that are at least one-third the diameter of the branch you are removing. Be sure to remove less than 25 percent of foliage at one time. It's best to thin trees in the winter, when they are dormant.

Heading back: Reduce the size of your tree this way by cutting back lateral branches and then heading tips of laterals.

Reduction cut: Most common in younger trees, these cuts remove an offshoot branch back to a thicker branch attached to the tree trunk. Pictured below is a cut to remove a perpendicular branch.

How to Prune a Tree

Start by undercutting from beneath the limb with your bow saw or chain saw.

Finish the cut from above. This keeps the bark from tearing when the limb breaks loose.

Trim the stub from the limb so it's flush with the branch collar.

Planting Trees

TOOLS & MATERIALS

Shovel	Long stake
Garden hose	Tree
Utility knife	Peat moss

Trees and shrubs are structural elements that provide many benefits to any property. Aside from adding structural interest to a landscape, they work hard to provide shade, block wind, and form walls and ceilings of outdoor living areas. Whether your landscape is a blank canvas or you plan to add trees and shrubs to enhance what's already there, you'll want to take great care when selecting what type of tree you plant, and how you plant it.

A substantially sized tree might be your greatest investment in plant stock, which is more reason to be sure you give that tree a healthy start by planting

it correctly. Timing and transportation are the first issues you'll consider. The best time to plant is in spring or fall, when the soil is usually at maximum moistness and the temperature is moderate enough to allow roots to establish. When you choose a tree or shrub, protect the branches, foliage, and roots from wind and sun damage during transport. When loading and unloading, lift by the container or rootball, not the trunk. You may decide to pay a nursery to deliver specimens if they are too large for you to manage, or if you are concerned about damaging them en route to your property.

Trees and shrubs are packaged three different ways for sale: with a bare root, container-grown, and balled-and-burlapped. Bare root specimens (left) are the most wallet-friendly, but you must plant them during the dormant season, before growing begins. Container-grown plants (center) are smaller and take years to achieve maturity, but you can plant them any time—preferably during spring or fall. Balled-and-burlapped specimens (right) are mature and immediately fill out a landscape. They are also the most expensive.

How to Plant a Balled-and-Burlapped Tree

Use a garden hose to mark the outline for a hole that is at least two or three times the diameter of the rootball. If you are planting trees with shallow, spreading roots (such as most evergreens) rather than a deep taproot, make the hole wider. Dig no deeper than the height of the rootball.

Amend some of the removed soil with hydrated peat moss and return the mixture to build up the sides of the hole, creating a medium that is easy for surface roots to establish in. If necessary (meaning, you dug too deep) add and compact soil at the bottom of the hole so the top of the rootball will be slightly above grade when placed.

Place the tree in the hole so the top of rootball is slightly above grade and the branches are oriented in a pleasing manner. Cut back the twine and burlap from around the trunk and let it fall back into the hole. Burlap may be left in the hole—it will degrade quickly. Non-degradable rootball wrappings should be removed.

Backfill amended soil around the rootball until the soil mixture crowns the hole slightly. Compress the soil lightly with your hands. Create a shallow well around the edge of the fresh soil to help prevent water from running off. Water deeply initially and continue watering very frequently for several weeks. Staking the tree is wise, but make sure the stake is not damaging the roots.

Planting Windbreaks

Wind saps heat from homes, forces snow into burdensome drifts, and can damage more tender plants in a landscape. To protect your outdoor living space, build an aesthetically pleasing wall—a "green" wall of tress and shrubs—that will cut the wind and keep those energy bills down. Windbreaks are commonly used in rural areas where sweeping acres of land are a runway for wind gusts. But even those on small, suburban lots will benefit from strategically placing plants to block the wind.

Essentially, windbreaks are plantings or screens that slow, direct, and block wind from protected areas. Natural windbreaks are comprised of shrubs, conifers, and deciduous trees. The keys to a successful windbreak are: height, width, density, and orientation. Height and width come with age. Density depends on the number of rows, type of foliage, and gaps. Ideally, a windbreak should be 60 to 80 percent dense. (No windbreak is 100 percent dense.) Orientation involves placing rows of plants at right angles to the wind. A rule of thumb is to plant a windbreak that is ten times longer than its greatest height. And keep in mind that wind changes direction, so you may need a multiple-leg windbreak.

A stand of fast-growing trees, like these aspens, will create an effective windbreak for your property just a few years after saplings are planted.

WINDBREAK BENEFITS

Windbreaks deliver multiple benefits to your property.

Energy conservation: reduce energy costs from 20 to 40 percent.

Snow control: single rows of shrubs function as snow fences.

Privacy: block a roadside view and protect animals from exposure to passers-by.

Noise control: muffle the sound of traffic if your pasture or home is near a road.

Aesthetic appeal: improve your landscape and increase the value of your property.

Erosion control: prevent dust from blowing; roots work against erosion.

TOOLS & MATERIALS

Shovel	Trees
Garden hose	Soil amendments
Utility knife	(as needed)

How to Plant a Windbreak

Before you pick up a shovel, draw a plan of your windbreak, taking into consideration the direction of the wind and location of nearby structures. Windbreaks can be straight lines of trees or curved formations. They may be several rows thick, or just a single row. If you only have room for one row, choose lush evergreens for the best density. Make a plan.

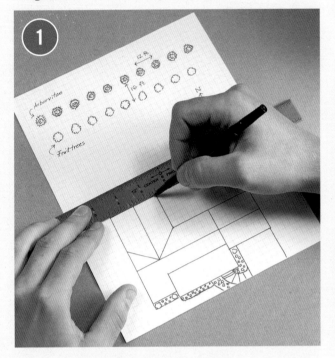

Once you decide on the best alignment of trees and shrubs, stake out reference lines for the rows. For a three-row windbreak, the inside row should be at least 75 ft. from buildings or structures, with the outside row 100 to 150 ft. away. Within this 25 to 75 ft. area, plant rows 16 to 20 ft. apart for shrubs and conifers and no closer than 14 ft. for deciduous trees. Within rows, space trees so their foliage can mature and eventually improve the density.

Dig holes for tree rootballs to the recommended depth (see page 37). Your plan should arrange short trees or shrubs upwind and taller trees downwind. If your windbreak borders your home, choose attractive plants for the inside row and buffer them with evergreens or dense shrubs in the second row. If you only have room for two rows of plants, be sure to stagger the specimens so there are no gaps.

Plant the trees in the formation created in your plan. Follow the tree and shrub planting techniques on page 37. Here, a row of dwarf fruit trees is being planted in front of a row of denser, taller evergreens (Techny Arborvitae).

Planting Annuals

An annual is any plant that completes its life cycle in one growing season. The term "annual" is usually used to refer to long-blooming flowering plants, many of which hail from tropical areas. These flowers have the ability to bring instant gratification anywhere they are placed—from your doorstep to the mailbox at the end of the driveway. They are often used as exclamation points in a landscape.

Annuals come in almost any color imaginable, and most of their impact comes from their showy flowers. But this group of plants also offers a wide range of leaf colors, growth habits, and textures. You can use them in mixed plantings for a bouquet effect or in mass groupings where you want a large area of a single color. They make great container plants and are good anywhere you want an instant show. You will often see annuals named as part of a "series." Annuals that are part of a series all have similar growth characteristics but tend to have different flower colors.

Like vegetables, annuals can be classified as cool-season or warm-season plants based on their tolerance of cool air and soil temperatures. Cool-season annuals, which include pansies, snapdragons, and calendulas, do better in mild temperatures and can quickly deteriorate in hot weather. Warm-season annuals such as marigolds, zinnias, and impatiens grow and flower best in warm weather and do not tolerate any frost.

Planting a full bed of colorful annuals takes a bit of effort every spring, but the blossoms will delight you for most of the growing season. Interspersing the annual flowers with shrubs or even perennials gives a nice contrast and sense of composition.

BUYING ANNUALS

When purchasing annuals at a garden center, look for healthy seedlings that have not overgrown their growing containers. Don't buy them too early. These young plants require daily watering and regular fertilizing, and the garden center or nursery is much better able to give this regular care than you are at home. Plants like these bluebells purchased in a 3- or 4-inch pot will look beautiful almost immediately; for a more economical project, buy smaller seedlings in flats of six or more plants.

Growing Annuals

Most annuals prefer well-drained soil that is rich in organic matter. Add a 2- to 4-inch layer of compost and mix it into the top 8- to 12-inches of soil the first year, adding a 1- to 2-inch layer of compost before planting in subsequent years. You can cover the bed with organic mulch, such as shredded bark, pine straw, or cocoa bean hulls, to reduce moisture evaporation and suppress weed growth. Just make sure the mulch doesn't overwhelm the small plants and adds to their beauty rather than detracting from it.

Some larger-seeded annuals are easy to start from direct seeding. These include cosmos, marigold, morning glory, nasturtium, sunflower, and zinnia. Smaller-seeded annuals such as petunia, impatiens, and lobelia are more difficult to sow and require longer growing times before they flower. They need to be started indoors or purchased as plants in spring in order to get flowers by midsummer.

Most warm-season annuals should be seeded indoors 6 to 8 weeks before the last spring frost, but some require 10 to 12 weeks or more. Tender annuals should not be planted outdoors until all danger of spring frost has passed. Even if they are not injured by low temperatures, they will not grow well until the soil warms. Cool-season annuals will tolerate lower temperatures, but even they don't like a hard frost. They can usually be planted outdoors about a week or two before the last expected spring frost date.

Plants started inside or purchased from a garden center need to be hardened off before planting them outdoors. Move the plants outside to a sheltered spot for a few hours, taking them back inside at night. Increase the outside time a little each day. After about a week, the plants should be tough enough to plant outdoors.

ANNUALS THAT AREN'T ANNUAL

There are some plants that are called "annuals" even though they technically live more than one year. Biennials, those plants that complete their life cycle in 2 years, are usually grouped with annuals. Hollyhocks and Canterbury bells, both technically biennials, will bloom their first year if set out early enough. Tender perennials such as geraniums and verbenas are also usually treated as annuals, even though they will survive from year to year in mild-winter climates. Because they are quick to bloom like true annuals, they are usually grown for one season and thrown out at the end. Lantana is an example of a woody shrub that is often grown as an annual in cold climates.

Foxglove (*Digitalis purpurea*) is a biennial, meaning it doesn't flower until its second summer after seeding. But it is often grouped with annuals in references and at nurseries.

Tips for Planting Annuals

To remove annual seedlings, gently pop the young plants from their cell-packs by squeezing the bottoms and pushing up. Do not grab plants by their tender stems or leaves.

When planting annuals, plant at the same depth they were growing in the containers. If your growing medium is properly prepared, it will be loose enough that you can easily dig shallow planting holes with your fingers. For gallon pots, use a trowel, spade, or cultivator.

Plants growing in peat pots can be planted pot and all, but remove the upper edges of peat pots so that the pot will not act as a wick, pulling water away from the roots.

Pinch off any flowers or buds so the plant can focus its energy on getting its roots established rather than flowering, then water well.

Care of Annuals

Weeding. Weeding is probably the biggest maintenance chore with annuals; these plants do not compete well with weeds. Keep garden beds weed free by pulling regularly or covering the soil with organic mulch. Remember to keep the mulch away from the plants' stems.

Watering. Most annuals need at least 1 to 1½ inches of water per week from rain or irrigation. More may be needed during very hot weather and as the plants get larger. Water thoroughly and deeply to promote strong root growth. Allow the soil surface to dry before watering again. Soaker hoses and drip irrigation that apply water directly to the soil are best. Overhead irrigation destroys delicate blooms and can contribute to many fungi and molds. Watering is best when completed in the morning hours, so foliage has a chance to dry before cooler evening temperatures set in.

Feeding. Annuals put a lot of energy into blooming and require regular applications of nutrients. An easy way to provide annuals with the nutrients they need is to use a slow-release, or time-released, fertilizer at planting time. One application will slowly release nutrients with every watering. Although these fertilizers cost more than other types, they are usually worth the investment to save yourself from having to apply biweekly liquid fertilizer applications. The newer annuals require high soil fertility to do their best. Apply a slow-release fertilizer at planting time, mixing it in with the soil, and plan to follow up with biweekly applications of a water-soluble fertilizer.

Grooming. Because they are only around for a few months, most annuals don't require a lot of grooming. Some of the taller types may need staking or support systems of some type. Staking is best done at planting time to avoid damaging roots. Some annuals benefit from pinching to promote bushiness. This list includes petunias and chrysanthemums. In general, pinching any plant that has become too leggy or too tall will make it bushier and more compact. One grooming task almost all annuals will benefit from is deadheading.

DEADHEADING

Deadheading is the process of removing spent flowers from annual plants to help stimulate prolonged and repeated blooming. Although tedious and completely optional, it is a good idea for a number of reasons. Removing spent flowers encourages rebloom, eliminates seed production and self-seeding, and makes your garden and landscape look a lot nicer. Cut back to the next set of leaves to encourage new buds to open.

Pruning can invigorate some species. Petunias can be cut back in midsummer to within a few inches of the ground, fertilized and heavily watered, and they will be full and attractive again in just a few weeks.

Planting Perennials

A plant that is perennial will survive more than one year, and technically can include trees, shrubs, grasses, bulbs, and even some vegetables. In gardening, the term "perennial" is usually used to describe herbaceous flowering plants that are grown specifically for their ornamental beauty. Typical perennials include daylilies, hostas, delphiniums, and yarrow.

Unlike annuals, perennials do not bloom throughout the growing season. Their bloom period can range anywhere from a week to a month or more. Many people shy away from perennials because of their higher initial cost. The extensive choices can also be overwhelming. But the fact that perennials live on from year to year provides several advantages. You will save the labor, time, and expense involved in replanting every year. Your garden will have continuity and a framework to work within. But the most appealing thing about using perennials is the astonishing array of colors, shapes, sizes, and textures available.

The tops of herbaceous perennials often die in the fall, but the roots survive the winter and send up new growth during the spring. Some herbaceous perennials grow a rosette of foliage (small leaves that

For home landscaping, the term perennial is typically used to mean flowering plants that return anew every growing season after dying back at the end of the previous growing period.

grow along the base of the plant, similar to what biennials grow) after the stems die off.

Perennials can be divided into evergreen and deciduous. Perennials that keep their foliage all year-round are evergreen perennials. Deciduous perennials lose their foliage during the fall or winter and produce new top growth in spring.

Perennials are a very diverse and versatile group of plants. There are perennials that will thrive in every soil type, from full sun to full shade. This sunny border includes daylilies, chrysanthemums, and coneflowers.

Creating a Perennial Border

As versatile as perennials are, the spot where they really shine is in a perennial border. A perennial border is a wonderful way to bring beauty to your landscape and enjoy these fascinating plants throughout the year. The goal with a perennial border is to create a garden with interest from early spring through fall, and even into the winter. A border is usually more interesting if it contains a wide variety of heights, colors, and textures, but some beautiful borders can be created with all one-color plants or with a target peak bloom time, such as spring.

The trick to designing a beautiful perennial border is to select plants that bloom at different times so you have something blooming throughout the growing season. This may take you a few seasons to master, but it is quite gratifying when it all comes together. Select a mix of early, mid-, and late bloomers that match your soil and sunlight conditions.

With a little planning, your perennial border can have something going on from early spring through fall, as in this garden, which includes coneflower, rudbeckia, astilbe, and violas.

Comprising common but beautiful perennial plants, the border garden seen here frames the relaxing lawn nicely. Included in the garden are iris, hosta, daylily, and daisy.

Planting Perennials

Most perennials are best planted in spring so they have an entire growing season to develop roots and become established before they have to face winter. Rainfall is also usually more abundant in spring. But container-grown plants can be planted almost any time during the growing season, as long as you can provide them with adequate moisture. If you plant in the heat of summer, you may need to provide some type of shading until the plants become established. Fall planting should be finished at least 6 weeks before hard-freezing weather occurs. Early spring is a good time to plant perennials in colder climates.

Plant spacing depends on each individual species and how long you want to wait for your garden to fill in, but generally about 12 inches is good for most herbaceous perennial plants. Obviously the more plants you can afford the sooner your garden will be more attractive and the fewer weed problems you will have. However, planting too densely can be a waste of money and effort.

Good soil preparation is extremely important for perennials, since they may be in place for many years. Dig the bed to a depth of 8 to 10 inches and work in at least 2 inches of organic matter before planting.

A cottage garden is a charming way to incorporate perennials into a landscape. It typically has a looser, more relaxed style and usually includes a lot of old-fashioned and fragrant flowers. It is a good style for people who like to have a lot of different plants.

Select a variety of perennials with varying bloom times, flower colors, and plant heights, as well as a few plants with interesting foliage to fill in.

How to Plant Perennials

Before removing plants from their containers, place them in the prepared garden to see how they will look together. Experiment with different groupings until you find an arrangement that pleases you.

Dig a hole about twice as wide as each container and deep enough so the plant is just a little higher than it was in the container, to allow for soil settling. Dig holes one at a time to make it easier to maintain the arrangement.

Gently remove the plant from its container and pull apart any circling roots. Fill in with soil and tamp it around the plant.

Water the entire garden thoroughly to settle the soil around the roots. Make sure the plants get plenty of water until they are established.

TIP: Create a shallow well ringing around the base of the stem to trap water so it doesn't run off as quickly.

Creating a New Garden Bed

Chances are there is already something growing where you want to install your new garden. And chances are it's not desirable vegetation. As tempting as it is, do not just jump right in and start planting, figuring it will be easy to just pull the weeds as you go. Proper site preparation is the key to success. Take the time to get rid of existing vegetation and improve the soil before you start putting plants in the ground. This preparation will pay significant dividends.

TOOLS & MATERIALS

Garden hose	Landscape edging
Spade	Landscape spikes
Newspapers or cardboard (optional)	Maul
Spray herbicide (optional)	Garden rake
Soil amendments	Mulch

How to Create a New Garden Bed

Use a sun-warmed garden hose to lay out your proposed garden, following the topography of the site. Most gardens look best with gentle curves rather than straight lines.

1

TIP: Smother the existing vegetation in the garden bed area with about 6" of organic mulch such as straw, shredded bark, or compost. Mow closely in the spring, then cover the area with a thick layer of newspaper or cardboard and then add the organic mulch. Keep the newspaper and mulch in place all summer. Replenish the mulch in fall, and by the next spring your garden should be ready for planting. This method works best on lawn areas rather than areas with lots of deep-rooted perennial weeds.

Remove existing vegetation. There are several ways to get rid of existing vegetation. Which way you choose depends on how much time you have and how you feel about using herbicides. The most natural way to create a new garden bed is to dig it up manually. Just be sure to get rid of all the existing plant roots. Even tiny pieces of tough perennial-weed roots can grow into big bad weeds in no time. A major disadvantage with this method is that you lose substantial amounts of topsoil. To avoid this, if you have the time, you can simply turn the sod over and allow it to decay on site. This will take at least one growing season.

Once the existing vegetation is dead or removed, turn the soil by hand or with a tiller, and add soil amendments. Do not use a tiller without killing all existing vegetation first—it may look like you've created a bare planting area, but all you've done is ground the roots into smaller pieces that will sprout into more plants than you started with. Even after multiple tillings spaced weeks apart, you'll be haunted by these root pieces.

Install landscape edging to keep lawn grasses from invading your garden. The best option is to install a barrier of some type. When it comes to barriers, it's worth paying more for a quality material. Metal edging buried 4" or more into the soil effectively keeps turf from sneaking in. If you go with black plastic edging, use contractor grade to avoid having to replace it in a few years.

Cover the new garden with mulch. Mulching your new garden will not only help keep the weeds from settling in, it will also help maintain soil moisture and prevent the soil from washing away until you can get the plants established. Cover the entire prepared garden bed with 2" to 3" of an organic mulch such as shredded bark, pine bark nuggets, cocoa bean hulls, or shredded leaves. Avoid using grass clippings; they tend to mat down and become smelly.

Concrete Curb Edging

Poured concrete edging is perfect for curves and custom shapes, especially when you want a continuous border at a consistent height. Keeping the edging low to the ground (about 1 inch above grade) makes it work well as a mowing strip, in addition to a patio or walkway border. Use fiber-reinforced concrete mix, and cut control joints into the edging to help control cracking.

Concrete edging draws a sleek, smooth line between surfaces in your yard and is especially effective for curving paths and walkways.

TOOLS & MATERIALS

Rope or garden hose	Circular saw	Concrete edger	Fiber-reinforced concrete
Excavation tools	Drill	1 × 1 wood stakes	Acrylic concrete sealer
Mason's string	Concrete mixing tools	¼" hardboard	Eye and ear protection
Hand tamp	Margin trowel	1" wood screws	Work gloves
Maul	Wood concrete float		

How to Install Concrete Curb Edging

Lay out the contours of the edging using a rope or garden hose. For straight runs, use stakes and mason's string to mark the layout. Make the curb at least 5" wide.

Dig a trench between the layout lines 8" wide (or 3" wider than the finished curb width) at a depth that allows for a 4"-thick (minimum) curb at the desired height above grade. Compact the soil to form a flat, solid base.

Stake along the edges of the trench, using 1" × 1" × 12" wood stakes. Drive a stake every 18" along each side edge.

Build the form sides by fastening 4"-wide strips of ¼" hardboard to the insides of the stakes using 1" wood screws. Bend the strips to follow the desired contours.

Add spacers inside the form to maintain a consistent width. Cut the spacers from 1 × 1 to fit snugly inside the form. Set the spacers along the bottom edges of the form at 3-ft. intervals.

Fill the form with concrete mixed to a firm, workable consistency. Use a margin trowel to spread and consolidate the concrete.

Tool the concrete: once the bleed water disappears, smooth the surface with a wood float. Using a margin trowel, cut 1"-deep control joints across the width of the curb at 3-ft. intervals. Tool the side edges of the curb with an edger. Allow to cure. Seal the concrete, as directed, with an acrylic concrete sealer, and let it cure for 3 to 5 days before removing the form.

Mulching Beds

Mulch is the dressing on a landscape bed, but its benefits run deeper than surface appeal. Mulch protects plant and tree roots, prevents soil erosion, discourages weed growth, and helps the ground retain moisture. You can purchase a variety of mulches for different purposes. Synthetic mulches and stones are long-lasting, colorful, and resist erosion. They'll never break down. Organic mulches, such as compost and wood chips, enrich soil and double as "dressing" and healthy soil amendments.

No matter what type of mulch you choose, application technique is critical. If you spread it too thick it may become matted down and can trap too much moisture. Too thin, it can wash away to reveal bare spots. If it is unevenly applied, it will appear spotty.

Consider timing before you apply mulch. The best time to mulch is mid- to late-spring, after the ground warms up. If you apply mulch too soon, the ground will take longer to warm up and your plants will suffer for it. You may add more mulch during the summer to retain water, and in the winter to insulate soil. (As weather warms, lift some of the mulch to allow new growth to sprout.) Spring is prime mulching time.

Mulch comes in many varieties, but most is made from shredded wood and bark. Because it is an organic material, it breaks down and requires regular refreshing.

How to Landscape with Mulch

Remove weeds from the bed and water plants thoroughly before applying mulch. For ornamental planting beds it often is a good idea to lay strips of landscape fabric over the soil before mulching.

OPTION: Help contain the mulch in a confined area by installing flexible landscape edging.

Working in sections, scoop a pile of material from the load (wheelbarrow or bag) and place the piles around the landscape bed.

Spread mulch material to a uniform 1" thickness to start. Do not allow mulch to touch tree trunks or stems of woody ornamentals. Compost can double as mulch and a soil amendment that provides soil with nutrients. If you don't make your own compost, you can purchase all-natural products such as Sweet Peet.

Rain Garden

A rain garden collects and filters water runoff, which prevents flooding and protects the environment from pollutants carried by urban stormwater. Rain gardens provide a valuable habitat for birds and wildlife, and these purposeful landscape features also enhance the appearance of your yard. In fact, when a rain garden is installed and planted properly, it looks like any other landscape bed on a property. (There are no ponds or puddles involved.) The difference is, a rain garden can allow about 30 percent more water to soak into the ground than a conventional lawn.

Though a rain garden may seem like a small environmental contribution toward a mammoth effort to clean up our water supply and preserve aquifers, collectively they can produce significant community benefits. For instance, if homeowners in a subdivision each decide to build a rain garden, the neighborhood could avoid installing an unsightly retention pond to collect stormwater runoff. So you see, the little steps you take at home can make a big difference.

Most of the work of building a rain garden is planning and digging. If you recruit some helpers for the manual labor, you can easily accomplish this project in a weekend. As for the planning, give yourself good time to establish a well-thought-out design that considers the variables mentioned here. And as always, before breaking ground, you should contact your local utility company or digging hotline to be sure your site is safe.

TOOLS & MATERIALS

Shovels

Rakes

Trowels

Carpenter's level

Small backhoe (optional)

Tape measure

Wood stakes, at least 2 ft. long

String

6 ft. 2 × 4 board (optional)

BEFORE YOU DIG

Determine the best place for your rain garden by answering the following questions:

- Where does water stand after a heavy rain?

- What is the water source? (drainpipe, runoff from a patio or other flat surface, etc.)

- What direction does water move on your property?

- Where could water potentially enter and exit a rain garden?

- Where could a rain garden be placed to catch water from its source before it flows to the lowest point on the property?

- Do you need more than one rain garden?

Preparing the Land

Soil is a key factor in the success of your rain garden because it acts as a sponge to soak up water that would otherwise run off and contribute to flooding, or cause puddling in a landscape. Soil is either sandy, silty, or clay based, so check your yard to determine what category describes your property. Sandy soil is ideal for drainage, while clay soils are sticky and clumpy. Water doesn't easily penetrate thick, compacted clay soils, so these soils need to be amended to aerate the soil body and give it a porous texture that's more welcoming to water runoff. Silty soils are smooth but not sticky and absorb water relatively well, though they also require amending. Really, no soil is perfect, so you can plan on boosting its rain garden potential with soil amendments. The ideal soil amendment is comprised of: washed sharp sand (50 percent); double-shredded hardwood mulch (15 percent); topsoil (30 percent); and peat moss (5 percent). Compost can be substituted for peat moss.

While planning your rain garden, give careful consideration to its position, depth, and shape. Build it at least 10 feet from the house, and not directly over a septic system. Avoid wet patches where infiltration is low. Shoot for areas with full or partial sun that will help dry up the land, and stay away from large trees. The flatter the ground, the better. Ideally, the slope should be less than a 12 percent grade.

Residential rain gardens can range from 100 to 300 square feet in size, and they can be much smaller, though you will have less of an opportunity to embellish the garden with a variety of plants. Rain gardens function well when shaped like a crescent, kidney, or teardrop. The slope of the area where you're installing the rain garden will determine how deep you need to dig. Ideally, dig 4 to 8 inches deep. If the garden is too shallow, you'll need more square footage to capture the water runoff, or risk overflow. If the garden is too deep, water may collect and look like a pond. That's not the goal.

Finally, as you consider the ideal spot for your rain garden—and you may find that you need more than one—think about areas of your yard that you want to enhance with landscaping. Rain gardens are aesthetically pleasing, and you'll want to enjoy all the hard work you put into preparing the land and planting annuals and perennials.

How to Build a Rain Garden

Choose a site, size, and shape for the rain garden, following the design standards outlined on the previous two pages. Use rope or a hose to outline the rain garden excavation area. Avoid trees and be sure to stay at least 10 ft. away from permanent structures. Try to choose one of the recommended shapes: crescent, kidney, or teardrop.

Dig around the perimeter of the rain garden and then excavate the central area to a depth of 4" to 8". Heap excavated soil around the garden edges to create a berm on the three sides that are not at the entry point. This allows the rain garden to hold water in during a storm.

Dig and fill sections of the rain garden that are lower, working to create a level foundation. Tamp the top of the berm so it will stand up to water flow. The berm eventually can be planted with grasses or covered with mulch.

Level the center of the rain garden and check with a long board with a carpenter's level on top. Fill in low areas with soil and dig out high areas. Move the board to different places to check the entire garden for level.

NOTE: If the terrain demands, a slope of up to 12 percent is okay. Then, rake the soil smooth.

Plant specimens that are native to your region and have a well-established root system. Contact a local university extension or nursery to learn which plants can survive in a saturated environment (inside the rain garden). Group together bunches of three to seven plants of like variety for visual impact. Mix plants of different heights, shapes, and textures to give the garden dimension. Mix sedges, rushes, and native grasses with flowering varieties. The plants and soil cleanse stormwater that runs into the garden, leaving pure water to soak slowly back into the earth.

Apply double-shredded mulch over the bed, avoiding crowns of new transplants. Mulching is not necessary after the second growing season. Complement the design with natural stone, a garden bench with a path leading to it, or an ornamental fence or garden wall. Water a newly established rain garden during drought times—as a general rule, plants need 1" of water per week. After plants are established, you should not have to water the garden. Maintenance requirements include minor weeding and cutting back dead or unruly plant material annually.

Xeriscape

Xeriscaping, in a nutshell, is waterwise gardening. It is a form of landscaping using drought-tolerant plants and grasses. How a property is designed, planted, and maintained can drastically reduce water usage if xeriscape is put into practice. Some think that xeriscaping will become a new standard in gardening as water becomes a more precious commodity and as homeowners' concern for the environment elevates.

Several misconceptions about xeriscaping still exist. Many people associate it with desert cactus and dirt, sparsely placed succulents and rocks. They are convinced that *turf* is a four-letter word and grass is

TOOLS & MATERIALS

Basic tools	Fill

far too thirsty for xeriscaping. This is not true. You can certainly include grass in a xeriscape plan, but the key is to incorporate turf where it makes the most sense: children's play areas or front yards protected from foot traffic. Also, your choice of plants expands far beyond prickly cactus. The plant list, depending on where you live, is long and varied.

Xeriscaping is associated with sand, cacti, and arid climates, but the basic idea of planting flora that withstands dry conditions and makes few demands on water resources is a valid goal in any area.

The Seven Principles of Xeriscape

Keep in mind these foundational principles of xeriscape as you plan a landscape design. First begin by finding out what the annual rainfall is in your area. What time of year does it usually rain? Answering these questions will help guide plant selection. Now look at the mirco-environment: your property. Where are there spots of sun and shade? Are there places where water naturally collects and the ground is boggy? What about dry spots where plant life can't survive? Where are trees, structures (your home), patios, walkways, and play areas placed? Sketch your property and figure these variables into your xeriscape design.

Also, carefully study these seven principles and work them into your plan.

1. **Water conservation:** Group plants with similar watering needs together for the most efficient water use. Incorporate larger plantings that provide natural heating and cooling opportunities for adjacent buildings. If erosion is a problem, build terraces to control water runoff. Before making any decision, ask yourself: how will this impact water consumption?

2. **Soil improvement:** By increasing organic matter in your soil and keeping it well aerated, you provide a hardy growing environment for plants, reducing the need for excess watering. Aim for soil that drains well and maintains moisture effectively. Find out your soil pH level by sending a sample away to a university extension or purchasing a home kit. This way, you can properly amend soil that is too acidic or alkaline.

3. **Limited turf areas:** Grass isn't a no-no, but planting green acres with no purpose is a waste. The typical American lawn is not water-friendly— just think how many people struggle to keep their lawns green during hot summers. If you choose turf, ask a nursery for water-saving species adapted to your area.

4. **Appropriate plants:** Native plants take less work and less water to thrive. In general, drought-resistant plants have leaves that are small, thick, glossy, silver-gray, or fuzzy. These attributes help plants retain water. As a rule, hot, dry areas with south and west exposure like drought-tolerant plants; while north- and east-facing slopes and walls provide moisture for plants that need a drink more regularly. Always consider a plant's water requirements and place those with similar needs together.

5. **Mulch:** Soil maintains moisture more effectively when its surface is covered with mulch such as leaves, coarse compost, pine needles, wood chips, bark, or gravel. Mulch will prevent weed growth and reduce watering needs when it is spread 3 inches thick.

6. **Smart irrigation:** If you must irrigate, use soaker hoses or drip irrigation (see page 43). These systems deposit water directly at plants' roots, minimizing runoff and waste. The best time to water is early morning.

7. **Maintenance:** Sorry, there's no such thing as a no-maintenance lawn. But you can drastically cut your outdoor labor hours with xeriscape. Just stick to these principles and consider these additional tips: 1) plant windbreaks to keep soil from drying out (see page 38); 2) if possible, install mature plants that require less water than young ones; 3) try "cycle" irrigation where you water to the point of seeing runoff, then pause so the soil can soak up the moisture before beginning to water again.

RANGE OF AVERAGE ANNUAL MINIMUM TEMPERATURES FOR EACH ZONE	
Zone 1	Below -50°F
Zone 2	-50°F to -40°F
Zone 3	-40°F to -30°F
Zone 4	-30°F to -20°F
Zone 5	-20°F to -10°F
Zone 6	-10°F to 0°F
Zone 7	0°F to 10°F
Zone 8	10°F to 20°F
Zone 9	20°F to 30°F
Zone 10	30°F to 40°F
Zone 11	40°F to 50°F

How to Xeriscape Your Yard

Plan the landscape with minimal turf, grouping together plants with similar water requirements. Refer to the Seven Principles of Xeriscape as you sketch (see page 59). Always consider your region's climate and your property's microclimate: rainfall, sunny areas, shady spots, wind exposure, slopes (causing run-off), and high foot-traffic zones.

Divide your xeriscape landscape plan into three zones. The oasis is closest to a large structure (your home) and can benefit from rain runoff and shade. The transition areas is a buffer between the oasis and arid zones. Arid zones are farthest away from structures and get the most sunlight. These conditions will dictate the native plants you choose.

Plant in receding layers by installing focal-point plants closest to the home (or any other structure), choosing species that are native to the area. As you get farther away from the home, plant more subtle varieties that are more drought tolerant.

As you plant beds, be sure to group together plants that require more water so you can efficiently water these spaces.

Incorporate groundcover on slopes, narrow strips that are difficult to irrigate and mow, and shady areas where turf does not thrive. Install hardscape such as walkways, patios, and steppingstone paths in high foot-traffic zones.

Mulch will help retain moisture, reduce erosion, and serves as a pesticide-free weed control. Use it to protect plant beds and fill in areas where turf will not grow.

Plant turf sparingly in areas that are easy to maintain and will not require extra watering. Choose low-water-use grasses adapted for your region. These may include Kentucky Bluegrass, Zoysia, St. Augustine, and Buffalo grass.

OPTION: Install a drip irrigation system to water plants efficiently.

Zen Garden

TOOLS & MATERIALS

Stakes

Mason's string

Garden hose

Landscape marking paint

Straight 2 × 4

Level

Measuring tape

Compactable gravel

Excavating tools

Crushed granite (light colored)

Hand maul

Manual tamper

Landscape fabric

Fieldstone steppers

Specimen stones

Border stones

Eye protection and work gloves

What's commonly called a Zen garden in the West is actually a Japanese dry garden, with little historical connection to Zen Buddhism. The form typically consists of sparse, carefully positioned stones in a meticulously raked bed of coarse sand or fine gravel. Japanese dry gardens can be immensely satisfying. Proponents find the uncluttered space calming and the act of raking out waterlike ripples in the gravel soothing and perhaps even healing. The fact that they are low maintenance and drought resistant is another advantage.

Site your garden on flat or barely sloped ground away from messy trees and shrubs (and cats), as gravel and sand are eventually spoiled by the accumulation of organic matter. There are many materials you can use as the rakable medium for the garden. Generally, lighter-colored, very coarse sand is preferred—it needs to be small enough to be raked into rills yet large enough that the rake lines don't settle out immediately. Crushed granite is a viable medium. Another option that is used occasionally is turkey grit, a fine gravel available from farm supply outlets. In this project, we show you how to edge your garden with cast pavers set on edge, although you may prefer to use natural stone blocks or even smooth stones in a range of 4 to 6 inches.

A Zen garden is a small rock garden, typically featuring a few large specimen stones inset into a bed of gravel. It gets its name from the meditative benefits of raking the gravel.

How to Make a Zen Garden

Lay out the garden location using stakes and string or hoses and then mark the outline directly onto the ground with landscape paint.

Excavate the site and install any large specimen stones that require burial more than ½ ft. below grade.

Dig a trench around the border for the border stones, and lay down landscape fabric.

Pour a 3" thick layer of compactable gravel into the border trench and tamp down with a post or a hand tamper.

(continued)

Place border blocks into the trench and adjust them so the tops are even.

5

6

Test different configurations of rocks in the garden to find an arrangement you like. If it's a larger garden, strategically place a few flat rocks so you can reach the entire garden with a rake without stepping in the raking medium.

7

Set the stones in position on individual beds of sand about 1" thick. Pour in pebbles.

8

Rake the medium into pleasing patterns with a special rake (see next page).

Once you have constructed your Zen garden, you will use two tools to interact with it: your eyes and a good rake. While any garden rake will suffice for creating the swirling and concentric rills that are hallmarks of the Zen garden, a special rake that's dedicated to the garden will enhance your hands-on interaction.

Many Zen garden rakes are constructed from bamboo. Bamboo is lightweight and readily available, especially through Internet sites. While you can certainly choose this material, you're likely to find that the lightness can actually work against it, causing you to exert more strain to cut through the raking medium. A rake made from solid wood has greater heft that lets it glide more smoothly through the medium. The rake shown here is made using only the following materials:

- 1¼"-dia. by 48" oak or pine dowel (handle)

- ½" by 36" oak or pine dowel (tines)

- 2" × 3" × 9½" piece of red oak (head)

Figure 1

Figure 2

Figure 3

Start by sanding all of the stock smooth using sandpaper up to 150 grit in coarseness. Soften the edges of the 2 × 3 with the sandpaper. Drill a 1¼" dia. hole in the head for the handle (Figure 1). The hole should go all the way through the head at a 22½° downward angle (half of a 45° angle), with the top of the hole no closer than ¾" to the top of the head. Use a backer board when drilling to prevent blowout and splinters.

Next, drill ½"-dia. by 1"-deep seat holes for the tines in the bottom edge of the blank. Locate centers of the two end holes 1" from the ends. Measure in 2½" from each end hole and mark centers for the intermediate tines. Use masking tape to mark a drilling depth of 1" on your drill bit and then drill perpendicular holes at each centerline. Cut four 5"-long pieces of the ½"-dia. oak doweling for the tines. Apply wood glue into the bottom of each hole and insert the tines, setting them by gently tapping with a wood mallet (Figure 2). Then, apply glue to the handle hole's sides and insert the handle so the end protrudes all the way through. After the glue dries, drill a ½"-dia. hole down through the top of the head and into the handle. Glue a ½" dowel into the hole to reinforce the handle (this is called pinning).

Finally, use a back saw, gentleman's saw, or Japanese flush-cutting saw to trim the handle end and the handle pin flush with the head (Figure 3). Sand to smooth the trimmed ends and remove any dried glue. Finish with two or three light coats of wipe-on polyurethane tinted for red oak.

Native plants are those species that grew naturally in an area before the greatest influx of European settlement, about the mid-1800s in most areas of North America. Native plants tend to lend themselves to less formal gardens, but many of them can also be used in formal settings as well.

There are many benefits to using native plants. For many gardeners, the initial attraction comes from native plants' reputation of being lower maintenance than a manicured lawn and exotic shrubs. For the most part this is true—provided native plants are given landscape situations that match their cultural requirements. Because they have evolved and adapted to their surroundings, native plants tend to be tolerant of tough conditions such as drought and poor soil and are better adapted to local climatic conditions and better able to resist any negative effects of insects and diseases.

The less tangible—but possibly more important—side of using native plants, is the connection you make with nature. Gardening with natives instills an understanding of our natural world—its cycles, changes, and history. By observing native plants throughout the year, a gardener gains insight into seasonal rhythms and life cycles. You will see an increase in birds, butterflies, and pollinating insects, making your garden a livelier place.

To find out what plants were native in your area, check out your state's Department of Natural Resources website, which often includes a list of native plants or links where you can find them. Your agricultural extension office can be helpful as well.

Native plants and natural gardens tend to be more informal and loosely structured, but they can also work fine in smaller, more formal settings with the right plant selection and planting techniques.

BOULEVARD GARDENS

There are many good reasons to garden on the boulevard: that narrow area between the municipal sidewalk and the street. In denser urban areas the space offers additional gardening square footage where it is often scarce. From an environmental standpoint, a boulevard garden creates a buffer for the street and sewer system, and the absence of clippings created by mowing a traditional grass boulevard helps keep unnecessary organic matter and lawn fertilizer out of the sewer system. Often, boulevards are left to "go native" by planting prairie grasses and other hardy, indigenous plants. More frequently these days, homeowners are truing to these strip areas to plant edibles.

Before you plant a boulevard garden, you should check with your municipality to see if there are restrictions you need to be aware of—these are usually related to height and sightline issues, as well as the need to maintain access from the street. Also, if you live in areas where the streets are plowed in the winter, it's likely that the soil on your boulevard contains high levels of road salt. This may limit your plant selection: inquire at your local garden center about plants that are salt tolerant.

Tips for Boulevard Gardening

- Good soil drainage is key since you need the water to percolate down rather than run off.

- Keep your soil line slightly below the sidewalk and curb heights to make sure no soil washes away.

- It's usually best to stick with low-growing clumping plants, but wider boulevards can handle shrubs and even small trees.

- Make sure your plants don't block people's ability to see at intersections.

- Stay away from prolific self-seeders; even a couple extra plants can make this small space look weedy.

Boulevard strips, or tree lawns as they are sometimes called, are the narrow areas between the sidewalk and the street. As prevalent as they are in urban landscapes, boulevards are often neglected when it comes to gardening. This is unfortunate since they are in plain view of anyone who visits or passes by on the sidewalk.

Pathways

Think of a pathway as a natural narrator. It tells the colorful story that draws people into your outdoor space. Sure, you can leave to chance the discovery of all the beauty and varied features of the backyard you've worked so hard to create. Or you can use a pathway to gently lead visitors to your annuals bed, prize roses, water feature, arroyo and bridge, garden bench, or gazebo.

The takeaway about the projects in this chapter— beyond that they generate immense gratification and a quick transformation of your outdoor area—is they are easy to pull off. They require negligible maintenance, make your yard look established and stately, and they protect your plants from those musing meanderers who might mangle your marigolds. While these pathways projects are not difficult, they do require a design and knowledge of materials, base drainage, and borders. All in all, it's a fun chapter with projects that promise to make your outdoor space inspiring and moving (literally).

In this chapter:
- Designing Paths & Walkways
- Loose Rock Landscape Path
- Steppingstone Landscape Path
- Cast Concrete Steppers
- Arroyo
- Classic Garden Bridge

Designing Paths & Walkways

The purpose of paths and walkways in the landscape is twofold: to visually connect various "rooms" and features; and to map out sensible, accessible, and comfortable walk routes from point A to point B—that is, from patio to garden, from sidewalk to front porch. A utilitarian approach is to lay a path for safety reasons, creating a clear-cut pedestrian runway that is meant to purposefully usher people to a destination. But many paths are much more than a means to an end. Your path will communicate to visitors where to go and how to get there. A less formal path will encourage a slower pace, forcing exploration. Steppingstones artfully placed in a garden will merely suggest a trail through a crowd of plant life. You'll eventually find the treasure at the end of the trail—prize roses, a gurgling fountain. The pleasure is in the journey.

While designing a path and considering materials for these projects, consider the experience you want people to have as they navigate the walkway. Do you want to guide them quickly without distraction, or do you hope they'll discover a cozy sitting area along the way? With your goals in mind, you can begin to sketch a road map.

Think of a path as a mini highway system for your yard. You may only require a single walkway that leads from a side garage door, around the house, to the deck out back. Or, your landscape design may include pockets of interest that you want people to discover: a pond, gazebo, bench, garden, or children's play area. In this case, you'll need some "side streets" or back roads. Your main artery will probably serve as a safe route with the sheer purpose of clearing the way for pedestrians. Pathways may branch off of this key walkway. These are the scenic byways.

A pebble pathway contained by a loose-laid brick border provides just enough tracking for people to safely meander through a woodland backyard.

Mixing materials can lead to very interesting and pleasing pathway designs, provided it is done with some discretion and design savvy. The loose gravel and flagstone pathway above has a distinct organic quality and a sense of relaxation and flow. The smaller pathway (inset) cobbled together from sections of old railroad ties, rocks and shells certainly is unique, but there is little to tie the elements together visually. In addition, the irregular walking surface created by the short, perpendicularly laid ties and the fairly large rocks does present a tripping hazard. With pathways and steps, surprises are best avoided.

A steppingstone walkway allows grass "grout" to grow. A path is important for guiding the eye, and foot traffic, through a landscape.

Color outside the lines. A straight line is a safe and efficient form for a pathway, but adding a few jogs and bends adds great visual interest.

Materials

Choose materials and structure your paths according to their purpose and your design preferences. Brick, flagstone, concrete pavers, and gravel are popular choices for paths. Their surfaces aren't completely smooth, promoting skid resistance that allows for safe traction. If you opt for steppingstones, be sure you consider the natural stride of everyone who will use the path regularly. Placing them just an inch too far apart can trip up walkers. (You can walk across concrete with wet feet and measure your stride to determine functional steppingstone placement.) On the other hand, if you simply want to establish a less defined walking zone, you can play with the arrangement of steppingstones and create interesting designs.

Brick, flagstone, gravel, and concrete pavers are readily available and can be formal or casual, depending on how you design the path. For instance,

Suitable materials for pathways include interlocking pavers, cobblestones, flagstones, and gravel. For gravel pathways, choose small aggregates ⅜" to ¾". The texture looks appealing, and if you choose a variety of sizes and shapes the surface will stay in place. Interlocking pavers have shapes and protrusions that are designed to fit together and create a mechanical bond. Square and rectangular pavers and cobblestones are easier to lay out in a pathway. Flagstones can be laid in a solid pattern or used as steppingstones.

mortared flagstone tends to look somewhat formal, while flagstone set on sand does not. Lay flagstone on a prepared, earthen surface and you can plant rock-loving groundcover varieties such as creeping thyme and moss in between the cracks. Manufactured brick will offer a uniform, clean look. Natural brick has color variances. Recycled brick will blend well in mature landscapes and also provide a rustic look. Decorative steppingstones can jazz up a gravel path.

Before committing to a material for your walkway surface, ask yourself these questions:

- How regularly will you use this path?

- What other materials exist in your landscape? (Think patio, retaining walls, etc.)

- What materials will complement your home's architecture?

- Describe the setting: formal, casual, rustic-country, private, highly visible, etc.

- Who will walk on this path, and do they have special needs? (An even flagstone pathway is safer to traverse than a less uniform walkway of aggregate stone.)

TEST YOUR IDEAS

Before setting a project in stone, quite literally, test your projects by cutting models from scrap cardboard or even paper. For instance, when creating a steppingstone path, test layouts with cardboard templates before purchasing real stone. It is easy to miscalculate the quantity of materials required to complete a project. Same goes with size. You may be surprised how large a steppingstone must be to look substantial on your property. Meanwhile, as you use your cardboard steppers to lay out the path, test placement and be sure to arrange the stones to conform to your stride.

- What are the site conditions? Is the area particularly soggy and prone to puddling? (Stone gets slippery when wet. And wet stone is a welcome environment for moss, which compounds the slick factor.)

Base & Borders

We'll delve into the specifics of preparing the base for your path in later sections of this book, but for now let's underscore the importance of setting a solid foundation. Whether your path is purely for foot traffic or primarily a decorative statement (most often, the goal is both of these), you must take steps to secure the base and plan for drainage. You won't need to install culverts or hire the Army Corps of Engineers for this task. A simple half-inch slope from the center of your path to its edges will direct water away from the middle, preventing puddles and unsafe, slippery conditions. This is called crowning. You'll notice that your street is slightly crowned, directing water toward the curb

and into drainage grates. You will need a similar, much smaller-scale, system for you landscape path.

Next, consider how you will edge your path. A decorative border is optional, but it allows another opportunity to mix and match materials so as to marry the many different materials used throughout the landscape. For example, if your patio is composed of tumbled concrete pavers, but your home has stone accents, you can create a stone path with a brick border to bring the contrasting surfaces together. Play with the possibilities. Install a brick border along a gravel path, place native rock boulders alongside a sandstone path, or set stone slabs alongside a path of cobbled concrete pavers. Play with different textures and colors as well.

Aside from brick and stone, consider other ways to define your path. Hedges establish an attractive green border, while plastic edging available at home centers will do a fine job of preventing plants and turf from invading your walkway.

A tamped firm base with good drainage is vital to a successful pathway project. Compactible gravel makes an excellent base.

Pathways normally require a border to contain the surfacing material and create a mowing edge. Brick pavers can be laid flat or buried deeper on end (called soldier style).

Loose Rock Landscape Path

TOOLS & MATERIALS

Mason's string	Edging
Hose or rope	Spikes
Marking paint	Professional-grade landscape fabric
Excavation tools	
Garden rake	Compactable gravel
Plate compactor	Dressed gravel
Sod stripper or power sod cutter	Eye and ear protection
	Work gloves
Wood stakes	Circular saw
Lumber (1 × 2, 2 × 4)	Maul
Straight 2 × 4	

Loose-fill gravel pathways are perfect for stone gardens, casual yards, and other situations where a hard surface is not required. The material is inexpensive, and its fluidity accommodates curves and irregular edging. Since gravel may be made from any rock, gravel paths may be matched to larger stones in the environment, tying them in to your landscaping. The gravel you choose need not be restricted to stone, either. Industrial and agricultural byproducts, such as cinder and ashes, walnut shells, seashells, and ceramic fragments may also be used as path material.

For a more stable path, choose angular or jagged gravel over rounded materials. However, if your preference is to stroll throughout your landscape barefoot, your feet will be better served with smoother stones, such as river rock or pond pebbles. With stone, look for a crushed product in the ¼" to ¾" range. Angular or smooth, stones smaller than that can be tracked into the house, while larger materials are uncomfortable and potentially hazardous to walk on. If it complements your landscaping, use light-colored gravel, such as buff limestone. Visually, it is much easier to follow a light pathway at night because it reflects more moonlight.

Stable edging helps keep the pathway gravel from migrating into the surrounding mulch and soil. When integrated with landscape fabric, the edge keeps invasive perennials and trees from sending roots and shoots into the path. Do not use gravel paths near plants and trees that produce messy fruits, seeds, or other debris that will be difficult to remove from the gravel. Organic matter left on gravel paths will eventually rot into compost that will support weed growth.

A base of compactable gravel under the surface material keeps the pathway firm underfoot. For best results, embed the surface gravel material into the paver base with a plate compactor. This prevents the base from showing through if the gravel at the surface is disturbed. An underlayment of landscape fabric helps stabilize the pathway and blocks weeds, but if you don't mind pulling an occasional dandelion and are building on firm soil, it can be omitted.

Construction Details

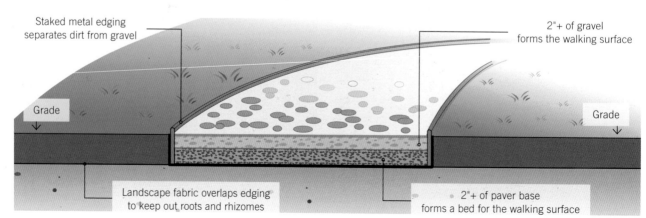

Staked metal edging separates dirt from gravel

2"+ of gravel forms the walking surface

Grade

Grade

Landscape fabric overlaps edging to keep out roots and rhizomes

2"+ of paver base forms a bed for the walking surface

Loose materials can be used as filler between solid surface materials, like flagstone, or laid as the primary groundcover, as shown here.

To ensure that the edges of the pathway are exactly parallel, create a spacer bar and use it as a guide to install the edging. Start with a piece of 2 × 4 that's a bit longer than the path width. Near one end, cut a notch that will fit snugly over the edging. Trim the spacer so the distance from the notch to the other end is the planned width of the pathway.

 How to Create a Gravel Pathway

Lay out one edge of the path excavation. Use a section of hose or rope to create curves, and use stakes and string to indicate straight sections. Cut 1 × 2 spacers to set the path width and establish the second pathway edge; use another hose and/or more stakes and string to lay out the other edge. Mark both edges with marking paint.

Remove sod in the walkway area using a sod stripper or a power sod cutter (see option, at right). Excavate the soil to a depth of 4" to 6". Measure down from a 2 × 4 placed across the path bed to fine-tune the excavation. Grade the bottom of the excavation flat using a garden rake.

NOTE: If mulch will be used outside the path, make the excavation shallower by the depth of the mulch. Compact the soil with a plate compactor.

OPTION: Use a power sod cutter to strip grass from your pathway site. Available at most rental centers and large home centers, sod cutters excavate to a very even depth. The cut sod can be replanted in other parts of your lawn.

Lay landscaping fabric from edge to edge, lapping over the undisturbed ground on either side of the path. On straight sections, you may be able to run parallel to the path with a single strip; on curved paths, it's easier to lay the fabric perpendicular to the path. Overlap all seams by 6".

Install edging over the fabric. Shim the edging with small stones, if necessary, so the top edge is ½" above grade (if the path passes through grass) or 2" above grade (if it passes through a mulched area). Secure the edging with spikes. To install the second edge, use a 2 × 4 spacer gauge that's been notched to fit over your edging (see facing page).

Stone or vertical-brick edges may be set in deeper trenches at the sides of the path. Place these on top of the fabric also. You do not have to use additional edging with paver edging, but metal (or other) edging will keep the pavers from wandering.

(continued)

Trim excess fabric, then backfill behind the edging with dirt and tamp it down carefully with the end of a 2 × 4. This secures the edging and helps it to maintain its shape.

Add a 2"- to 4"-thick layer of compactable gravel over the entire pathway. Rake the gravel flat. Then, spread a thin layer of your surface material over the base gravel.

Tamp the base and surface gravel together using a plate compactor. Be careful not to disturb or damage the edging with the compactor.

Fill in the pathway with the remaining surface gravel. Drag a 2 × 4 across the tops of the edging using a sawing motion, to level the gravel flush with the edging.

Set the edging brick flush with the gravel using a mallet and 2 × 4.

Tamp the surface again using the plate compactor or a hand tamper. Compact the gravel so it is slightly below the top of the edging. This will help keep the gravel from migrating out of the path.

Rinse off the pathway with a hose to wash off dirt and dust and bring out the true colors of the materials.

Steppingstone Landscape Path

A steppingstone path is both a practical and appealing way to traverse a landscape. With large stones as foot landings, you are free to use pretty much any type of fill material in between. You could even place steppingstones on individual footings over ponds and streams, making water the temporary infill that surrounds the stones. The infill does not need to follow a narrow path bed, either. Steppers can be used to cross a broad expanse of gravel, such as a Zen gravel panel or a smaller graveled opening in an alpine rock garden.

Steppingstones in a path serve two purposes: they lead the eye, and they carry the traveler. In both cases, the goal is rarely fast, direct transport, but more of a relaxing stroll that's comfortable, slow-paced, and above all, natural. Arrange the steppingstones in your walking path according to the gaits and strides of the people that are most likely to use the pathway. Keep in mind that our gaits tend to be longer on a utility path than in a rock garden.

TOOLS & MATERIALS

Mason's string	Landscape fabric
Hose or rope	Coarse sand
Marking paint	Thick steppers or broad river rocks with one flat face
Sod stripper	
Excavation tools	¼" to ½" pond pebbles
Hand tamp	2½"-dia. river rock
Wood stakes	Eye and ear protection
1 × 2 lumber	Work gloves
Straight 2 × 4	Level
Edging	Rake

Sometimes steppers are placed more for visual effect, with the knowledge that they will break the pacing rule with artful clusters of stones. Clustering is also an effective way to slow or congregate walkers near a fork in the path or at a good vantage point for a striking feature of the garden.

In the project featured here, landscape edging is used to contain the loose infill material (small aggregate), however a steppingstone path can also be effective without edging. For example, setting a series of steppers directly into your lawn and letting the lawn grass grow between them is a great choice as well.

CHOOSING STEPPERS

Select beefy stones (minimum 2½" to 3½" thick) with at least one flat side. Thinner steppingstones tend to sink into the pebble infill. Stones that are described as steppingstones usually have two flat faces. For the desired visual effect on this project, we chose steppers and 12" to 24" wide fieldstones with one broad, flat face (the rounded face is buried in the ground, naturally).

Fieldstone with a flat face

Steppers

Steppingstones blend beautifully into many types of landscaping, including rock gardens, ponds, flower or vegetable gardens, or manicured grass lawns.

How to Make a Pebbled Steppingstone Path

Excavate and prepare a bed for the path as you would for the gravel pathway (see pages 76 to 79), but use coarse building sand instead of compactable gravel for the base layer. Screed the sand flat so it's 2" below the top of the edging. Do not tamp the sand.

TIP: Low-profile plastic landscape edging is a good choice because it does not compete with the pathway.

Moisten the sand bed, then position the steppingstones in the sand, spacing them for comfortable walking and the desired appearance. As you work, place a 2 × 4 across three adjacent stones to make sure they are even with one another. Add or remove sand beneath the steppers, as needed, to stabilize and level the stones.

Pour in a layer of larger infill stones (2"-dia. river rock is seen here). Smooth the stones with a garden rake. The infill should be below the tops of the steppingstones. Reserve about one third of the larger diameter rocks.

Add the smaller infill stones, that will migrate down and fill in around the larger infill rocks. To help settle the rocks, you can tamp lightly with a hand tamper, but don't get too aggressive—the larger rocks might fracture easily.

Scatter the remaining large infill stones across the infill area so they float on top of the other stones. Eventually, they will sink down lower in the pathway and you will need to lift and replace them selectively to maintain the original appearance.

Variations

Move from a formal space to a less orderly area of your landscape by creating a pathway that begins with closely spaced steppers on the formal end and gradually transforms into a mostly-gravel path on the casual end, with only occasional clusters of steppers.

Combine concrete stepping pavers with crushed rock or other small stones for a path with a cleaner, more contemporary look. Follow the same basic techniques used on these two pages, setting the pavers first, then filling in between with the desired infill material(s).

Cast Concrete Steppers

Traditional walkway materials, such as brick and stone, have always been prized for both appearance and durability, but they can be expensive. As an easy and inexpensive alternative, you can build a new concrete path using prefabricated pathway forms. The result is a beautiful pathway that combines the custom look of brick or natural stone with the durability and economy of poured concrete.

Building a path is a great do-it-yourself project. Once you've prepared a base for the path, mix the concrete, fill and set the form, and lift the form to reveal the finished design. After a little troweling to smooth the surfaces, you're ready to create the next section using the same form. Simply repeat the process until the path is complete. Each form creates a section that's approximately 2 square feet using one 80-pound bag of premixed concrete.

DIY-friendly concrete casting forms are sold in several sizes and configurations. You simply lay them on a prepared surface, fill them with concrete, and remove them once the concrete has set; then, place the form next to the poured section and add another until your pathway is complete. Once all the concrete has dried, you can fill in the gaps between the pavers to further simulate the look of a genuine paver walkway.

TOOLS & MATERIALS

Excavation and site preparation tools
Concrete pathway form
Wheelbarrow or mixing box
Shovel

Level
Margin trowel or finishing trowel
Concrete mix or crack-resistant concrete mix

Liquid cement color
Plastic sheeting
Polymer-modified jointing sand

How to Estimate Concrete

ESTIMATING CONCRETE FOR COUNTRY STONE PATTERN (INTERLOCKS SO EACH SECTION IS APPROX. 1 FT. 9 IN.)

Length	# of Poured	# of 80-lb. Bags	# of 60-lb. Bags of walk
2 ft.	1	1	2
3 ft. 9 in.	2	2	3
5 ft. 6 in.	3	3	4
9 ft.	5	5	7
16 ft.	9	9	12
23 ft.	13	13	18
30 ft.	17	17	23

How to Make a Cast Concrete Path

Prepare the project site by removing sod or soil and excavating the pathway area. Level as needed and add 2" to 4" of compactible gravel to form a sub-base. The base should be a few inches wider than the planned pathway thickness.

Mix a batch of concrete for the first section. Adding colorant to the dry concrete mix gives the concrete the appearance of pavers or cobblestones. Note the ratio of colorant you add to the first batch of concrete so you can repeat it and maintain consistent color. The mixture should be fairly stiff so it holds its shape as it dries instead of slumping.

Place the form at the start of your path and level it. Shovel the wet concrete into the form to fill each cavity. Rap or bounce the form lightly to help settle the concrete. Drag a piece of 2 × 4 across the top in a zigzag motion to strike off the excess concrete.

Remove the form carefully. Test it first by slowly pulling up on the form to make sure the concrete will hold its shape. If it sags, press the form back down, let the concrete dry for a few minutes, and try again. Once you have removed the form, clean off any dried material and reposition it to pour the next section. Repeat as needed.

After removing each form, trowel the edges of the section to create the desired finish. For a nonskid surface, lightly brush the concrete with a broom or whisk broom before the concrete dries. Damp-cure the entire path for 5 to 7 days.

TIP: Pathway forms come in many shapes to create additional patterns, including this country stone pattern. Some, such as this, are better suited for curving pathways.

Variation: Quick-and-Easy Steppingstone Path

Place steppingstones in a desired pathway on your lawn.
Rotating the stones for jaunty angles and asymmetrical lines
is an easy way to liven up a backyard path. Steppingstones
are available in a wide variety of textures, shapes, and sizes,
so take the time to select what's right for your garden. Here,
natural stones on turf provide a useful and decorative accent.

Allow the steppingstones to remain on the lawn for several
days to kill the grass. This provides an outline for excavation
and makes turf removal much easier.

Dig around the outline for each stone and excavate the soil
or turf. To allow room for a layer of sand to stabilize the
steppingstone, dig each hole 2" deeper than the height of
the stone. Spread sand in each hole.

Place steppingstones in sand-filled holes, adding or removing
sand until each steppingstone is stable. Sand serves as
grout, filling in the small gaps between the hole and the
surrounding turf.

Casting your own concrete steppingstones is a great winter project. You can make a couple every week in your basement or garage. By the time spring arrives, you'll have enough to make a lengthy and unique steppingstone pathway. You can make a simple square, round or rectangular form from sheet stock (melamine coated particle board works well because concrete doesn't stick to it). Steppers should be at least 2 inches thick. Or, you might be able to find a readymade form laying around your house, such as a trash can lid. For extra strength you can add metal reinforcing mesh to the middle of the stepper, but unless you're making very large ones (2 square feet or more) it is probably not necessary.

How to Make DIY Cast Concrete Steppers

Make a form for your steppers by screwing wood strips to sheet stock. Or, you may find an item lying around the house that makes a suitable form, such as the cake pan in the inset photo. The form should be water-tight.

Spray a light coat of release agent onto the form (inset) and then fill it with a relatively stiff mixture of wet concrete, following the mixing instructions on the bagged concrete. To help the concrete settle into the form, vibrate it with a reciprocating saw that has no blade installed.

Strike off the excess concrete by dragging a piece of 2 × 4 across the surface in a sawing motion. The goal is to achieve a smooth surface with no bulges or voids.

Once the concrete sets up and the bleed water on the surface has evaporated, carefully brush the surface in a regular patter with a stiff-bristled broom. This process (called brooming) creates a nonskid surface. If you want a smoother finish, skim the concrete with a metal float or trowel instead of brooming it (inset).

Arroyo

An arroyo is a dry streambed or watercourse in an arid climate that directs water runoff on the rare occasions when there is a downfall. In a home landscape an arroyo may be used for purely decorative purposes, with the placement of stones evoking water where the real thing is scarce. Or it may serve a vital water-management function, directing storm runoff away from building foundations to areas where it may percolate into the ground and irrigate plants, creating a great spot for a rain garden. This water management function is becoming more important as municipalities struggle with an overload of storm sewer water, which can degrade water quality in rivers and lakes. Some communities now offer tax incentives to homeowners who keep water out of the street.

When designing your dry streambed, keep it natural and practical. Use local stone that's arranged as it would be found in a natural stream. Take a field trip to an area containing natural streams and make some observations. Note how quickly the water depth drops at the outside of bends where only larger stones can withstand the current. By the same token, note how gradually the water level drops at the inside of broad bends where water movement is slow. Place smaller river-rock gravel here, as it would accumulate in a natural stream.

Large heavy stones with flat tops may serve as step stones, allowing paths to cross or even follow dry streambeds.

The most important design standard with dry streambeds is to avoid regularity. Stones are never spaced evenly in nature, nor should they be in your arroyo. If you dig a bed with consistent width, it will look like a canal or a drainage ditch, not a stream. And consider other yard elements and furnishings. For example, an arroyo presents a nice opportunity to add a landscape bridge or two to your yard.

Important: Contact your local waste management bureau before routing water toward a storm sewer; this may be illegal.

An arroyo is a drainage swale lined with rocks that directs runoff water from a point of origin, such as a gutter downspout, to a destination, such as a sewer drain or a rain garden.

TOOLS & MATERIALS

Landscape paint	8"-thick steppers
Carpenter's level	6" to 18" dia.
Spades	river-rock boulders
Garden rake	¾" to 2" river rock
Wheelbarrow	Native grasses or other
Landscape fabric	perennials for banks
6-mil black plastic	Eye protection
Mulch	Work gloves

How to Build an Arroyo

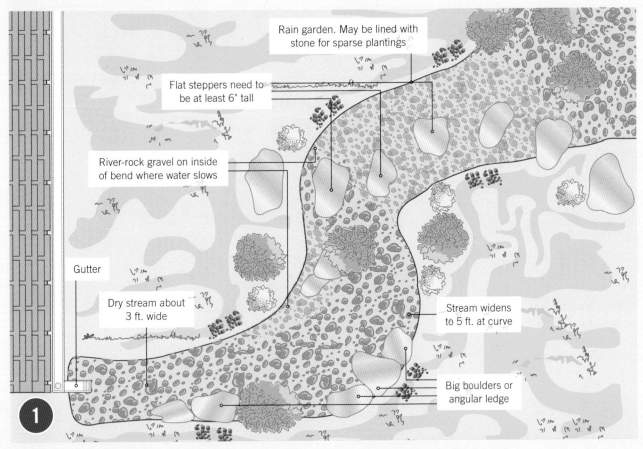

Rain garden. May be lined with stone for sparse plantings

Flat steppers need to be at least 6" tall

River-rock gravel on inside of bend where water slows

Gutter

Dry stream about 3 ft. wide

Stream widens to 5 ft. at curve

Big boulders or angular ledge

1

Create a plan for the arroyo. The best designs have a very natural shape and a rock distribution strategy that mimics the look of a stream. Arrange a series of flat steppers at some point to create a bridge.

2

Lay out the dry stream bed, following the native topography of your yard as much as possible. Mark the borders and then step back and review it from several perspectives.

3

Excavate the soil to a depth of at least 12" (30 cm) in the arroyo area. Use the soil you dig up to embellish or repair your yard. *(continued)*

Widen the arroyo in selected areas to add interest. Rake and smooth out the soil in the project area.

Install an underlayment of landscape fabric over the entire dry streambed. Keep the fabric loose so you have room to manipulate it later if the need arises.

Set larger boulders at outside bends in the arroyo. Imagine that there is a current to help you visualize where the individual stones could naturally end up.

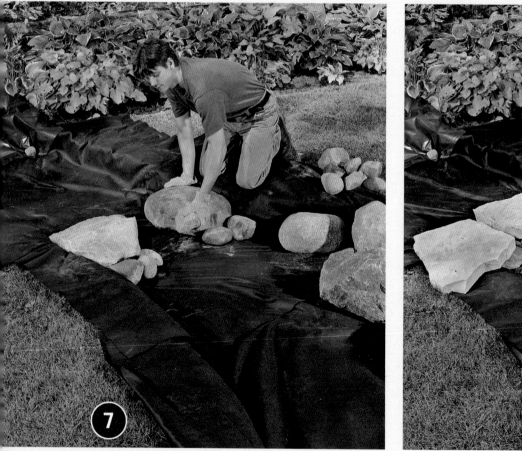

Place flagstone steppers or boulders with relatively flat surfaces in a steppingstone pattern to make a pathway across the arroyo (left photo). Alternately, create a "bridge" in an area where you're likely to be walking (right photo).

8 Add more stones, including steppers and medium-size landscape boulders. Use smaller aggregate to create the streambed, filling in and around, but not covering, the larger rocks.

Dress up your new arroyo by planting native grasses and perennials around its banks.

9

WHAT IS A RAIN GARDEN?

A rain garden is simply a shallow, wide depression at least 10 feet away from a basement foundation that collects storm water runoff. Rain gardens are planted with native flood-tolerant plants and typically hold water for only hours after rainfall. Check your local garden center or extension service to find details about creating rain gardens in your area (see page 54).

Classic Garden Bridge

An elegant garden bridge invites you into a landscape by suggesting you stop and spend some time there. Cross a peaceful pond, traverse an arroyo of striking natural stone, or move from one garden space to the next and explore. While a bridge is practical and functions as a way to get from point A to point B, it does so much more. It adds dimension, a sense of romanticism, and the feeling of escaping to somewhere special.

The bridge you see here can be supported with handrails and trellis panels, but left simple as pictured, its Zen appeal complements projects in this book, including: arroyo, garden pond, and rain garden. We think the sleek, modern design blends well in the landscape, providing a focal point without overwhelming a space.

TOOLS & MATERIALS

4" × 4" × 8' cedar (4)
2" × 10" × 8' cedar (2)
2" × 4" × 8' cedar (10)
1" × 8" × 8' cedar (2)
1" × 3" × 8' cedar (2)
1" × 2" × 8' cedar (8)
½" × 2" × 8' cedar lattice (2)
Lag screws (⅜" × 4")
Deck screws (2", 3")
Finishing materials
Jigsaw
Circular saw
Drill

Unlike many landscape and garden bridges that are large, ornate, and designed to be the center of attention, this low cedar bridge has a certain refined elegance that is a direct result of its simple design.

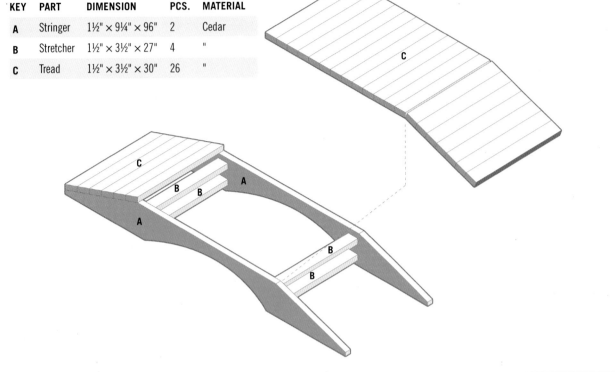

CLASSIC GARDEN BRIDGE

CUTTING LIST

KEY	PART	DIMENSION	PCS.	MATERIAL
A	Stringer	1½" × 9¼" × 96"	2	Cedar
B	Stretcher	1½" × 3½" × 27"	4	"
C	Tread	1½" × 3½" × 30"	26	"

Preparing Bridge Pieces

Study the cutting list carefully and take care when measuring for cuts. The building blocks of this bridge are: stringers, a base, and treads. Read these preliminary instructions carefully, then study the steps before you begin.

Stringers: This first step involves cutting the main structural pieces of the bridge. The stringers have arcs cut into their bottom edges, and the ends of stringers are cut at a slant to create a gradual tread incline. Before you cut stringers, carefully draw guidelines on the wood pieces:

- A centerline across the width of each stringer

- Two lines across the width of each stringer 24 inches to the left and right of the centerline

- Lines at the ends of each stringer, 1 inch up from one long edge

- Diagonal lines from these points to the top of each line to the left and right of the center

Base: Four straight boards called stretchers form the base that support the bridge. Before cutting these pieces, mark stretcher locations on the insides of stringers, 1½ inches from the top and bottom of the stringers. The outside edges of the stretchers should be 24 inches from the centers of the stringers so the inside edges are flush with the bottoms of the arcs. When working with the stretchers, the footboard may get quite heavy, so you will want to move the project to its final resting place and finish constructing the project there.

Treads: Cut the treads to size according to the cutting list. Once laid on the stringers, treads will be separated with ¼-inch gaps. Before you install the treads, test-fit them to be sure they are the proper size.

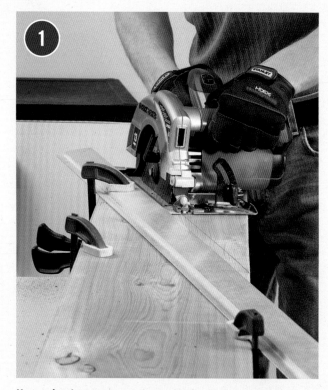

Use a circular saw to cut the ends of stringers along the diagonal lines, according to the markings described on the previous page.

Tack a nail on the centerline, 5¼" up from the same long edge. Also tack nails along the bottom edge, 20½" to the left and right of the centerline.

Make a marking guide from a thin, flexible strip of scrap wood or plastic, hook it over the center nail, and slide the ends under the outside nails to form a smooth curve. Trace along the guide with a pencil to make the arc cutting line.

Use a jigsaw to make arched cut-outs in the bottoms of the 2 × 10 stringers after removing the nails and marking guide.

Assemble the base by preparing stringers as described on facing page and positioning the stretchers between them. Stand the stringers upright (curve at the bottom) and support bottom stretchers with 1½"-thick spacer blocks for correct spacing. Fasten stretchers between stringers with countersunk 3" deck screws, driven through the stringers and into the ends of the stretchers.

Turn the stringer assembly upside down and attach the top stretchers.

Attach treads after test-fitting them. Leave a ¼" gap between treads. Secure them with 3"-long countersunk deck screws.

Sand all surfaces to smooth out any rough spots, and apply an exterior wood stain to protect the wood, if desired. You can leave the cedar untreated and it will turn gray, possibly blending with other landscape features.

Stone Walls

What is it about stone walls that inspire? Perhaps it is that they create boundaries and corral a wild, haphazard landscape. Perhaps it is they lend a sense of earthen timelessness and permanence to a landscape; they make a bold-but-natural statement that this outdoor area is well planned, graced with a touchstone structure even as plantings come and go.

Stone walls are more expensive and time-consuming to build than other types of walls, but they stand for decades as testimony to the builder's patience and craftsmanship. They weather well and require little maintenance. They blend with whatever you want to grow; indeed, their classy ruggedness is a dramatic, natural backdrop and a strikingly satisfying complement to the softness of plants. Finally, they serve as a seat for ruminating souls and a stage for container plants to put on their show.

In this chapter, you'll learn to design, build, and repair these beautiful barriers. There are many types, but we have chosen project plans for five stone walls that will set your landscape apart. One of the projects is unique in that it creates two-for-one beauty where there was a horrible mowing task; the steep-hill walls double as flower beds. If you're concerned that stone walls are too tough to build, don't be. You may want to round up a little help for some of the heavy lifting, but stacking stone is a project you can do yourself—especially with the step-by-step instructions, photos, and illustrations provided.

In this chapter:
- Designing Stone Walls
- Stone Wall Solution
- Stone-Terrace Accent Wall
- Interlocking Block Retaining Wall
- Drystack Garden Wall
- Mortared Garden Wall
- Repairing Stone Walls

Designing Stone Walls

Walls can accompany stairs, enclose a patio, or frame a garden—but they also can stand alone. Walls are a powerful design tool for creating physical and visual barriers. They can conceal unappealing yard features from the rest of the garden. They set limits, draw lines, divide property. They are an ample platform for growing vines, and if they're short enough, walls are handy overflow seating if you're hosting a large patio party.

When deciding on a wall style and material, consider the visual impact of this feature. Walls make a statement, and their appearance will set the tone in your landscape. A tidy brick-paver wall sends a different message than a dry stacked fieldstone structure. A wall composed of natural stone blends with the landscape.

Regarding materials, you can go natural with dry stacked fieldstone, ashlar (typical, blocky wall stone), or choose among an array of manufactured "interlocking" products.

Pre-cast landscape blocks and pavers are very easy to build with. Their interlocking features and uniform shape and size greatly ease the installation process.

A dry-stacked fieldstone wall can look as though it grew right out of the earth. Natural stone belongs in the environment, and it harmonizes with other natural landscape elements. Even without mortar holding the stones together, these walls can last for generations.

Garden Walls

Garden walls may be built using mortar to bind the stones, or they may be dry-stacked. Your climate, wall dimensions, and materials will dictate the best construction method. Mortared walls usually require a reinforced concrete footing poured below the frost line so the wall does not flex and crack at the joints. To further prevent freeze/thaw damage, keep water out of a mortar wall by topping the structure with capstones, which helps seal the top of the wall and thus limit water penetration. Mortar allows you to meld together interesting and rounded, decorative stones that need sticking power. Sealing seams between rock layers will not allow plants to peek through, which can be a pro or con, depending on your desire for the overall effect.

Not all walls require mortar, and you may prefer the aged-and-tumbled look of a dry-stacked wall. These walls do not require a poured concrete base since they can flex with the movement of the earth without cracking. Dry-stacked walls freely accommodate freeze-and-thaw cycles. Constructing such a wall is like piecing together a complex puzzle: no two pieces are truly a fit until you cut and rearrange stones, wedge shards into gaps, and artfully create a continuous surface. If you're not up for the challenge, you can hire a professional.

Tumbled concrete wall block can blend almost seamlessly with a patio or walkway made of similar material.

The classic stone garden wall recalls the origins of the building technique: as fields and pastures were cleared of rocks and impediments, the stones were simply stacked into short walls for storage. The walls also had the utilitarian job of keeping animals penned in and marking boundaries.

Retaining Walls

As the name suggests, a retaining wall holds back soil. In essence, a retaining wall turns a slope into a plateau-and-drop. Rather than a steep grade, you have a flat-planed surface supported by a sturdy wall. This allows you to readily use the flat space for planting, placing furniture, or even laying a patio. The dramatic drop adds interest and utility to a landscape. A common technique for long, sloped yards is to terrace several stepped-down retaining walls, creating earthen landings that break up the slope into manageable sections.

When building a stone retaining wall, you can use natural materials or interlocking blocks designed for the express purpose of stacking. Either can bear the weight of the heavy soil being retained, but cast blocks are DIY-friendly, durable, and easier on your wallet than natural stone. You can purchase interlocking blocks with natural finishes that blend better with the environment than some of the first-generation products did. You don't need to worry about shaping landscaping blocks because the flat tops and bottoms of interlocking blocks are smooth and ready to stack.

You can also go natural with materials and opt for ashlar that has been split into rectangular blocks. Stacked fieldstone accomplishes a rustic look. A row of boulders is an artistic way to create a boundary.

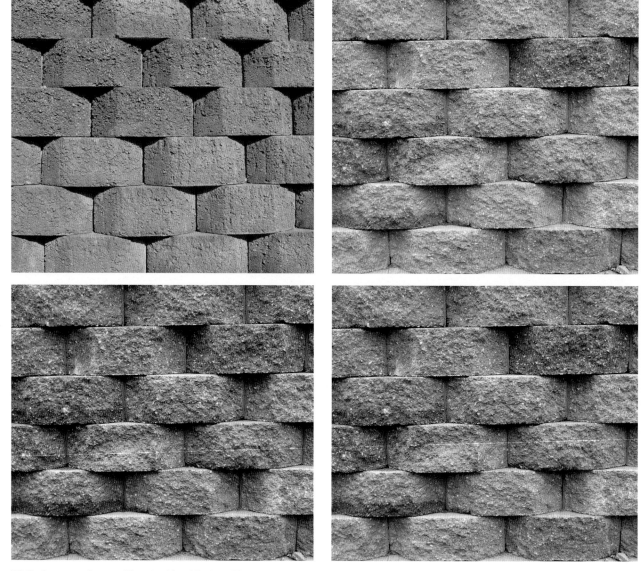

While few manufactured interlocking blocks will ever be mistaken for natural stone, the options in color, size, surface texture and shape have increased dramatically in recent years.

If slope is an issue along your wall site, you can easily build a stepped wall to accommodate it. The key is to keep the stones level so they won't shift or slide with the grade, and to keep the first course below ground level. This means digging a stepped trench.

Lay out the wall site with stakes and mason's string. Dig a trench 4 to 6 inches deep along the entire site, including the slope. Mark the slope with stakes at the bottom where it starts and at the top where it ends.

Begin the first course along the straight-line section of the trench, leading up to the start of the slope. At the reference stake, dig into the slope so a pair of shaping stones will sit level with the rest of the wall.

To create the first step, excavate a new trench into the slope, so that the bottom is level with the top of the previous course. Dig into the slope the length of one-and-a-half stones. This will allow one pair of stones to be completely below the ground level, and one pair to span the joint where the new trench and the stones in the course below meet.

Continue creating steps, to the top of the slope. Make sure each step of the trench section remains level with the course beneath. Then fill the courses, laying stones in the same manner as for a straight-line wall. Build to a maximum height of 36 inches, and finish by stepping the top to match the grade change, or create a level top with the wall running into the slope.

If you'd like a curved wall or wall segment, lay out each curve, as demonstrated on page 141. Then dig the trench as for a straight wall, sloping the sides into a slight V toward the center. Lay the stones as for a straight wall, but use shorter stones; long, horizontal stones do not work as well for a tight curve. Lay the stones so they are tight together, offsetting the joints along the entire stretch. Be careful to keep the stone faces vertical to sustain the curve all the way up the height of the wall.

To build a curved wall, lay out the curve using a string staked to a center point as a compass. Then, dig the trench and set stones using the same techniques as for a straight wall.

If the wall goes up- or downhill, step the trench, the courses, and the top of the wall to keep the stones level.

Stone Wall Solution

No matter how small your yard, mowing a steep slope can be a dreadful task. And if you're an avid gardener, you'd much rather groom a series of luscious planting beds than maneuver a lawnmower on a treacherous hill. That's why the front yard of this small, city lot was transformed with a series of beautiful stone walls. The following pages show you exactly how this landscape project was accomplished.

Although building a dry-stacked stone wall like this one is time-consuming, it does not require special masonry skills. And it is usually less strenuous than working with manufactured concrete landscape blocks, which are typically heavier than limestone.

TOOLS & MATERIALS

Pick	Mortar
Sledgehammer	Pointing trowel
Mason's hammer	Compactable gravel
Wrecking bar	sub-base (open-grade)
Mason's chisel	¾" gravel
Shovel or power	Drain tile
excavating equipment	Cut stone (ashlar)
Plate compactor	Cap stones
Bow rake	Work gloves
Tape measure	Eye protection
4-ft. level	

DESIGN VARIATION: Adding outcroppings. To help support mounds of soil and plants within each tier, place small boulders as outcroppings within the tiers. Strategically set to support the greatest elevation changes, these rocks are partially submerged in the soil to help them stay in position. In some spots, the wall stone can be shaped to wrap around the boulder (inset).

This limestone retaining wall blends naturally into the hillside and complements the bungalow house beyond.

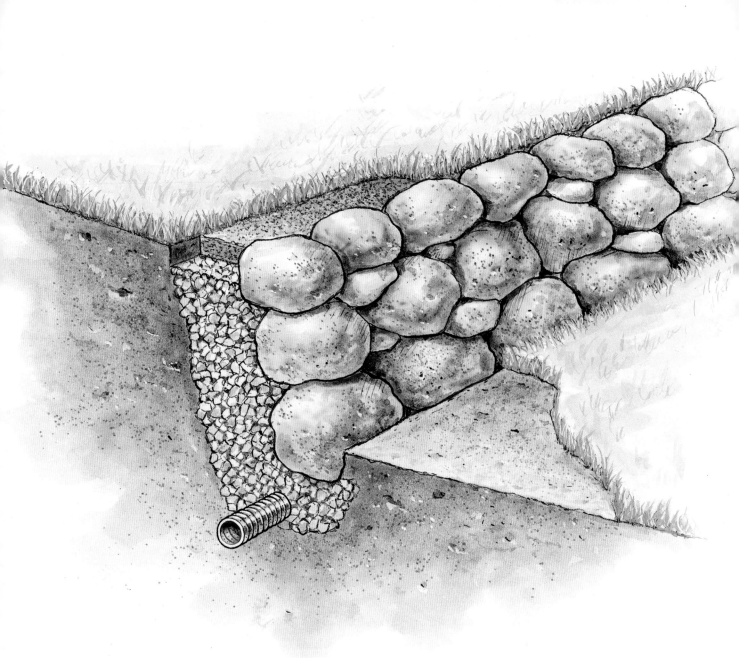

For any stone wall that is higher than 24", drain tile (surrounded by aggregate) must be installed.

PREPARATION TIPS

- Obtain a survey of your property to be sure your project fits within the boundaries.

- Dial 8-1-1 to have underground utilities marked.

- Tell your neighbors about the project beforehand; they'll be more tolerant of the mess or any inconvenience and noise if they're in on the plan.

- Check with your city regarding code requirements, setbacks, etc., and about street restrictions for deliveries of stone and gravel.

- Determine a convenient staging area for piling extra soil and supplies.

- Know your soil. Is it sand or clay?

- Collect all of the tools and gear you'll need before you begin.

DESIGN TIPS FOR DRY-STACK STONE RETAINING WALLS

- Only the top course is set in mortar; gravity holds the other stones in place.

- Buy "uniform" cut stone. In the dry-stacked wall featured here, the cut Chilton stones vary in thickness and length but are a uniform 8-inch width. Chilton is a type of limestone from Wisconsin that is available at most stone yards; you could also use other types of locally quarried limestone.

- For inspiration, look at stone walls in your area and check out stone suppliers' displays to find types of rock and designs that you like.

- Stagger joints between stones in overlaying courses.

- Use a scale drawing and the dimensions of the rise and span of the hill to calculate the wall's surface area; order 20 percent more stone than the plan requires to allow for waste. Don't forget to include the buried base layers of the walls in your calculations.

- Look at the house for patterns to mimic in the landscape. It's important to consider the entire composition.

- Incorporate arcs into the shape of the wall to give the natural-stone structure an organic, flowing design, but also to reflect and curves featured in the house.

- Use shrubs and plantings to help create visual balance for longer, non-straight walls.

- Each course of the wall must be made of stones of the same thickness. Aesthetically and structurally, it's best to use the thickest stones for the lower courses.

- To save installation time, sort the stones into piles according to their thickness, in ¼-inch increments, before starting the project.

- The maximum allowed height for a dry-stacked stone wall is 4 feet.

- Install buried drain tile (perforated drain pipe) if the wall height is more than 24 inches.

- When terracing a hill, always work from the bottom up.

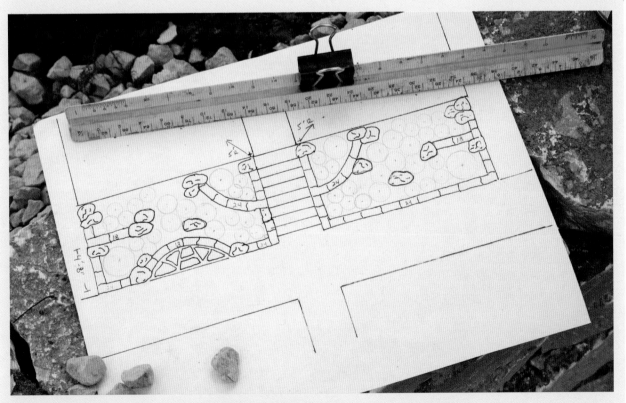

A scaled plan drawing of the retaining wall and the surrounding yard is a very important reference for doing professional-looking work.

How to Build a Dry-stack Stone Retaining Wall

Once your design is complete and has received any required municipal building permits, begin the excavation. For this wall, a 12"-wide × 7"-deep trench was dug along the edge of the sidewalk, with care taken not to disturb the soil below. Smooth the bottom of the trench, making sure it is level with the horizon (which is typically not parallel with the grade of the sidewalk). Then, spread a 2" layer of compactable ¾" open-grade gravel, which is angular and contains no crushed material. The angled surfaces of the stones help to lock them in place, preventing shifting, and the absence of crushed material allows water to drain more easily. Pack the 2" layer using a power plate compacter, the top of a maul or a tamper. Add another 2" of gravel and pack again, continuing until you have a smooth, level 4"-thick base. (The remaining 3" of trench depth allows the first course of stone to be below grade.)

TIP: A power plate compactor is faster and more effective than hand tamping, and you can rent one from most home centers and rental companies. They weigh nearly 200 pounds but move along easily when running. Wear hearing and eye protection, gloves, and reinforced-toe boots.

Lay the base course of rocks directly onto the compacted sub-base, following your plan. As with any wall construction, the base course sets the stage for the rest of the project. For this first layer, you can use stones that have odd shapes or different thicknesses, as long as the top surfaces are all even and level. Pound down any high spots using the top end of a maul: it is ideal for tamping down the high end of a stone or for packing smaller areas of gravel. The tool's weight and long handle make it easy to lift and drop, and the flat top works as a mini plate compacter. Check for level front-to-back and side-to-side. If you can't get it perfect, err on the side of a slightly higher front edge than back.

Install the next course, which should be fully above grade in most cases. As you install each stone, flip and turn it until you have a solid fit. You might need to try a different one for compatibility with neighboring stones and with the base. Set the front face of each new row ¼" back from the previous row (called the setback). Regardless of their finished height, stone walls require an 8"- to 10"-wide layer of ¾" gravel behind them. If your site has clay soil, which is prone to hydrostatic pressure and can cause any retaining wall to bulge and heave, use open-grade gravel (without crushed fines that harden when they dry) behind the wall to allow rain and melting snow to drain through.

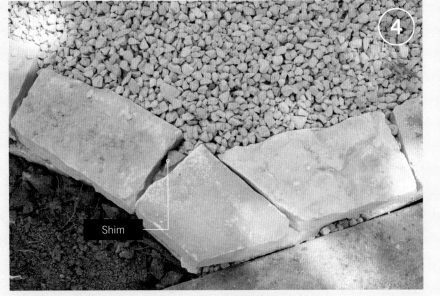

Shim

Put a stone sliver (shim) in any wedge-shape openings along the back sides; then fill behind it with gravel. The shim prevents gravel from passing through the spaces.

TIP: Keep a bucket of limestone chips handy to fill gaps and function as shims. These shims become tightly affixed under the weight of the wall.

Stabilize the stones. Natural stones' irregular shapes sometimes make a slight "rocking" movement unavoidable. You can compensate by shimming with a stone chip (called chinking) under the offending rock. Where needed, you can knock off protruding edges of stones with a maul. Try to avoid leaving gaps between neighboring stones, but where they occur, fill vertical spaces with a stone chip and gravel.

(continued)

Construct the return wall as you build so you can weave them into the courses of the main wall. The return walls (the sections that run alongside the steps and into the hill) need to extend into the soil at least 6" beyond their exposed portions. The hidden portions must also be supported with packed gravel and a course of base stone.

Each row of stones is stepped back (battered) ¼" along the front faces. It's a subtle graduation, apparent only when compared with a level. Battering adds significant strength to a dry-stacked wall. Use various sizes of levels to check each stone as you install it, adjusting for level front-to-back and side-to-side. Continue to backfill with gravel as you add each new course.

TIP: If your soil is very sandy, you can add landscape fabric between the gravel backfill and the soil behind it. Do not lay fabric directly against the back of the wall.

Install the top course using the longest, flattest stones you have (many stoneyards sell these stones separately as "capstones"). Avoid capstones that are more than 2" thick. Dry-lay and level the entire top course. Then, tip back each stone so you can set the top courses back into a 1"-thick bed of mortar applied to the rear halves of the surfaces of the stones below. This keeps the capstones from sliding or becoming otherwise displaced. Backfill with gravel: To allow room for a layer of soil and plants, stop adding gravel backfill when you're 5" shy of the top of the wall. You may choose to place landscape fabric on top of the gravel before adding the soil.

TIP: To prevent soil from seeping past the top layer of stone, you can pack mortar along the back of the capstone row as well.

CUTTING STONE

For most of your project, you likely will be able to pick through the stones to find a good fit, but sometimes you need a custom shape or size. You can use these methods for cutting stone:

- Chisel and hammer (score and tap along the score line with the chisel several times)

- Maul (whack and hope to get lucky)

- Diamond-blade gas saw (rental)

- Hydraulic splitter

Some stones have visible grain lines that may indicate where they are likely to split, but in most cases your results will depend on luck. You (and any bystanders or helpers) should always wear eye and hearing protection when cutting or breaking stone.

Retaining walls are only visible from one side; the back is flush against the grade and must withstand pressure from soil, especially when that soil gains even more poundage under wet conditions. With this in mind, larger retaining walls rely on behind-the-scenes elements like drain tile and gravel backfill for proper drainage and overall stability.

Examine the photo on this page. The drainage gravel behind the wall prevents soil from turning to mud and exerting pressure on the wall. Landscape fabric keeps soil from seeping into gravel, which is a sort of filter leading to the drain tile. If soil stops water from bleeding to the drain tile, you're back to the heavy-soil-mud-pressure problem. Drain tiles are installed with perforations facing down. One end of the drain tile is exposed so runoff can escape. Because dry-stacked walls bleed water through their faces, drainage tile is not always necessary.

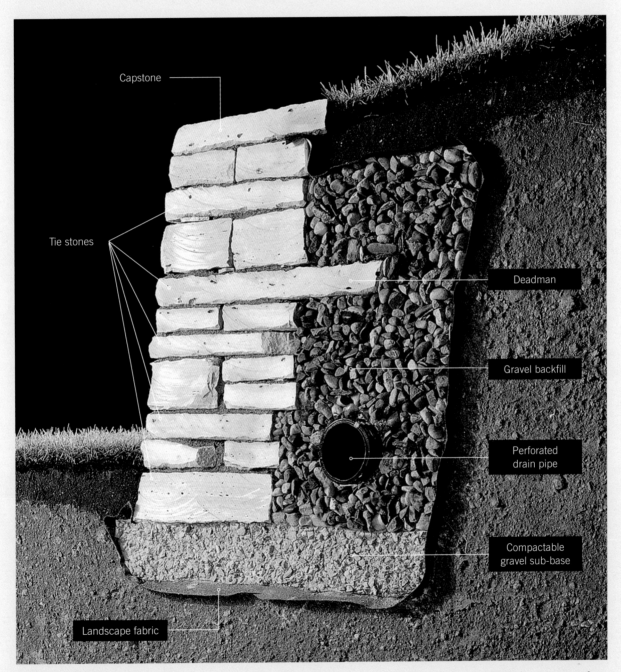

Capstone

Tie stones

Deadman

Gravel backfill

Perforated drain pipe

Compactable gravel sub-base

Landscape fabric

Stone retaining walls must contain several key design elements to allow for drainage and to hold back the pressure of the earth. "Deadmen" are long stones that are installed perpendicular to the wall and then extend back into the slope. River-rock backfill creates plenty of air pockets, facilitating good drainage. To further enhance drainage, drain tile (perforated pipe) may be laid near the bottom course of the wall.

Stone-Terrace Accent Wall

Rough-cut wall stones may be dry-stacked (without mortar) into retaining walls, garden walls, and other stonescape features. Dry-stack walls are able to move and shift with the frost, and they also drain well so they don't require deep footings and drainage tiles. Unlike fieldstone and boulder walls, short wall-stone walls can be just a single stone thick.

In the project featured here, we use rough-split limestone blocks about 8 by 4 inches thick and in varying lengths. Walls like this may be built up to 3 feet tall, but keep them shorter if you can, to be safe. Building multiple short walls is often a more effective way to manage a slope than to build one taller wall. Called terracing, this practice requires some planning. Ideally, the flat ground between pairs of walls will be approximately the uniform size.

A dry-laid natural stone retaining wall is a very organic-looking structure compared to interlocking block retaining walls (see page 118). One way to exploit the natural look is to plant some of your favorite stone-garden perennials in the joints as you build the wall(s). Usually one plant or a cluster of three will add interest to a wall without suffocating it in vegetation or compromising its stability. Avoid plants that get very large or develop thick, woody roots or stems that may compromise the stability of the wall.

A well-built retaining wall has a slight lean, called a batter, back into the slope. It has a solid base and the bottom course is dug in behind the lower terrace. Drainage gravel can help keep the soil from turning to mud, which will slump and press against the wall.

The same basic techniques used to stack natural stone in a retaining wall may be used for building a short garden wall as well. Obviously, there is no need for drainage allowances or wall returns in a garden wall. Simply prepare a base similar to the one shown here and begin stacking. The wall will look best if it wanders and meanders a bit. Unless you're building a very short wall (less than 18 inches), use two parallel courses that lean against one another for the basic construction. Cap it with flat capstones that run the full width of the wall (see page 114).

A natural stone retaining wall not only adds a stunning framework to your landscape, but it also lends a practical hand to prevent hillsides and slopes from deteriorating over time.

Cross-Sections: Stone Retaining Walls

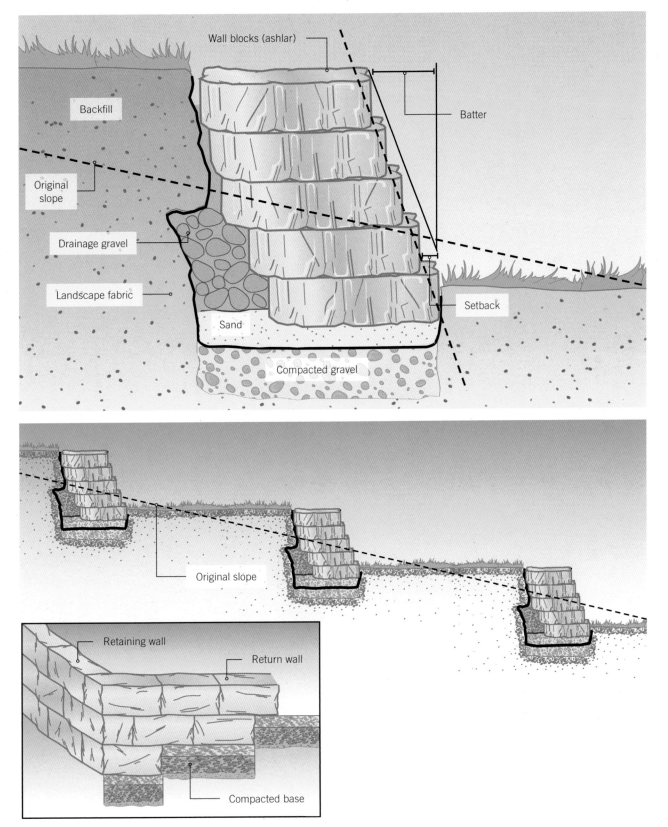

A stone retaining wall breaks up a slope to neat flat lawn areas that are more usable (top). A series of walls and terraces (bottom) break up larger slopes. Short return walls (inset) create transitions to the yard.

How to How to Build a Stone Retaining Wall

Dig into the slope to create a trench for the first wall. Reserve the soil you remove nearby—you'll want to backfill with it when the wall is done.

Level the bottom of the trench and measure to make sure you've excavated deeply enough.

After compacting a base, cover the trench and hill slope with landscape fabric, and then pour and level a 1" layer of coarse sand.

Place the first course of stones in rough position. Run a level mason's string at the average height of the stones.

Add or remove gravel under each stone to bring the front edges level with the mason's string.

Begin the second course with a longer stone on each end so the vertical gaps between stones are staggered over the first course.

Finish out the second course. Use shards and chips of stone as shims where needed to stabilize the stones. Check to make sure the ½" setback is followed.

Finish setting the return stones in the second course, making adjustments as needed for the return to be level.

(continued)

Backfill behind the wall with river rock or another good drainage rock.

Fold the landscape fabric over the drainage rock (the main job of the fabric is to keep soil from migrating into the drainage rock and out the wall) and backfill behind it with soil to level the ground.

Trim the landscape fabric just behind the back of the wall, near the top.

Finish the wall by capping it off with some of your nicer, long flat stones. Bond them with block-and-stone adhesive.

Level off the soil behind the wall with a garden rake. Add additional walls if you are terracing.

⑬

PLANTING YOUR RETAINING WALL

Natural stone retaining walls look quite lovely in their own right. However, you can enhance the effect by making some well-chosen planting choices for the wall itself. You can plan for this in the wall construction by leaving an extra wide gap between two stones in one of the courses and then planting in the gap. Or you can replace a stone in the wall with a shorter one, also creating a gap. To plant a gap, cut the fabric and set a good-size, bare-root perennial of an appropriate species to the bottom of this joint. Fan out the roots over the soil and use sphagnum moss to plug up the gaps in the wall around plants. Adhere the stone in the next course that bridges the gap with block-and-stone adhesive. Keep plants well watered until established. Eventually, the plant roots will hold the soil instead of the moss.

Set plants in natural-looking clusters of the same species. Do not suffocate the wall with too many plants.

Interlocking Block Retaining Wall

Think of retaining walls as shelves in your landscape where colorful plants can be on display, or as layers that carve nooks out of a sloped area to make the space more user-friendly. The fact is, keeping grass alive on a steep slope is virtually mission impossible. You can prevent erosion and form levels of usable space by building a retaining wall, or series of walls.

Retaining walls may be functional—serving to literally "retain" land at various levels on a slope; or purely aesthetic, as a way to add visual, vertical interest to a flat landscape. In this case, you'll be bringing in soil to backfill the retaining wall. Regardless of the reason for building a retaining wall, the materials available today make the job much like putting together a puzzle. You don't need mortar, and you can find interlocking block in various textures and colors that complement existing architectural features. Some types of block simply stack, while others are held together by an overlapping system of flanges. These flanges automatically set the backward pitch as blocks are stacked. Still, some blocks use fiberglass pins.

TOOLS & MATERIALS

Wheelbarrow	Tape measure
Shovel	Marking pencil
Garden rake	Caulk gun
Line level	Stakes
Hand tamper	Mason's string
Tamping machine	Landscape fabric
Small maul	Compactable gravel
Masonry chisel	Perforated drain pipe
Eye protection	Coarse backfill material
Hearing protectors	Construction adhesive
Work gloves	Retaining wall block
Circular saw with masonry-cutting blade	Cap blocks
Level	Spray paint

Terraced retaining walls work well on steep hillsides. Two or more short retaining walls are easier to install and more stable than a single, tall retaining wall. Construct the terraces so each wall is no higher than 3 ft.

Design Considerations

If your slope exceeds 4 feet in height, create a terrace effect with a series of retaining walls. Build the first retaining wall, then progress up the slope and build the next, allowing several feet between layers. The bleacher effect provides shelves for plantings and reduces erosion.

If your retaining wall will exceed 4 feet in height, consider bringing in a professional to assist with the job. The higher the wall, the more pressure—thousands of pounds—it must withstand from soil and water. Also, significant walls may require a building permit or specially engineered design. Keep in mind, interlocking block weights up to 80 pounds each, so you'll want to draft some helpers regardless of the project height. You can use cut stone rather than interlocking block and the project steps are the same. Both materials are durable and easy to work with.

Finally, tune into potential drainage issues before breaking ground. A wall can be damaged when water saturates the soil behind block or stone. You may need to dig a drainage swale in low-lying areas before beginning. This project includes a drainpipe to usher water away from the wall.

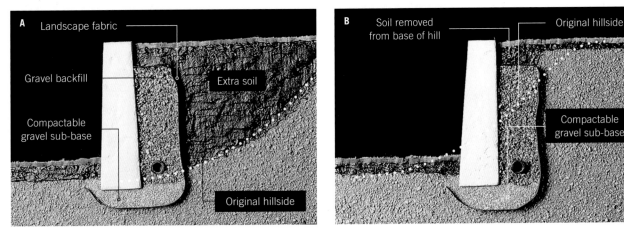

Increase the level area above the wall (A) by positioning the wall well forward from the top of the hill. Fill in behind the wall with extra soil, which is available from sand-and-gravel companies. Keep the basic shape of your yard (B) by positioning the wall near the top of the hillside. Use the soil removed at the base of the hill to fill in near the top of the wall.

BUILDING RETAINING WALLS

Backfill with crushed stone and install a perforated drainpipe about 6" above the bottom of the backfill. Vent the pipe to the side or bottom of the retaining wall, where runoff water can flow away from the hillside without causing erosion.

Make a stepped trench when the ends of a retaining wall must blend into an existing hillside. Retaining walls often are designed so the ends curve or turn back into the slope.

How to Build a Retaining Wall Using Interlocking Block

Interlocking wall blocks do not need mortar. Some types are held together with a system of overlapping flanges that automatically set the backward pitch (batter) as the blocks are stacked, as shown in this project. Other types of blocks use fiberglass pins (inset).

Pins

Overlapping flanges

Crushed stone backfill

First row installed upside down

Perforated drainpipe

Compactable gravel sub-base

Landscape fabric

Excavate the hillside, if necessary. Allow 12" of space for crushed stone backfill between the back of the wall and the hillside. Use stakes to mark the front edge of the wall. Connect the stakes with mason's string and use a line level to check for level.

Dig out the bottom of the excavation below ground level, so it is 6" lower than the height of the block. For example, if you use 6"-thick block, dig down 12". Measure down from the string to make sure the bottom base is level.

Line the excavation with strips of landscape fabric cut 3 ft. longer than the planned height of the wall. Make sure all seams overlap by at least 6".

(4)

Spread a 6" layer of compactable gravel over the bottom of the excavation as a sub-base and pack it thoroughly. A rented tamping machine, or jumping jack, works better than a hand tamper for packing the sub-base.

(5)

Lay the first course of block, aligning the front edges with the mason's string. (When using flanged block, place the first course upside down and backward.) Check frequently with a level, and adjust, if necessary, by adding or removing sub-base material below the blocks.

(6)

Lay the second course of block according to manufacturer's instructions, checking to make sure the blocks are level. (Lay flanged block with the flanges tight against the underlying course.) Add 3" to 4" of gravel behind the block and pack it with a hand tamper.

(7)

Make half-blocks for the corners and ends of a wall and use them to stagger vertical joints between courses. Score full blocks with a circular saw and masonry blade, and then break the blocks along the scored line with a maul and chisel. *(continued)*

Fill behind the wall with crushed stone and pack it thoroughly with the hand tamper. Lay the remaining courses of block, except for the cap row, backfilling with crushed stone and packing with the tamper as you go.

Add and tamp crushed stone, as needed, to create a slight downward pitch (about ¼" of height per foot of pipe) leading to the drainpipe outlet. Place the drainpipe on the crushed stone, 6" behind the wall, with the perforations face down. Make sure the pipe outlet is unobstructed. Lay courses of block until the wall is about 18" above ground level, staggering the vertical joints.

Before laying the cap block, fold the end of the landscape fabric over the crushed stone backfill. Add a thin layer of topsoil over the fabric, and then pack it thoroughly with a hand tamper. Fold any excess landscape fabric back over the tamped soil.

Apply landscape construction adhesive to the top course of block, and then lay the cap block. Use topsoil to fill in behind the wall and to fill in the base at the front of the wall. Install sod or plants as desired.

How to Add a Curve to an Interlocking Block Retaining Wall

Right angle

Excavate for the wall section, following the curved layout line. To install the first course of landscape blocks, turn them upside down and backwards and align them with the radius curve. Use a 4-ft. level to ensure the blocks sit level and are properly placed.

Outline the curve by first driving a stake at each end and then driving another stake at the point where lines extended from the first stakes would form a right angle. Tie a mason's string to the right-angle stake, extended to match the distance to the other two stakes, establishing the radius of the curve. Mark the curve by swinging flour or spray paint at the string end, like a compass.

Use half blocks or cut blocks to create finished ends on open ends of the wall.

Install subsequent courses so the overlapping flange sits flush against the back of the blocks in the course below. As you install each course, the radius will change because of the backwards pitch of the wall, affecting the layout of the courses. Where necessary, trim blocks to size. Install using landscape construction adhesive, taking care to maintain the running bond.

Dry-stack Garden Wall

TOOLS & MATERIALS

Mason's string and stakes	Trowel
Compactable gravel	Stiff-bristle brush
Ashlar stone	Work gloves
Capstones	Protective footwear
Mortar mix	

Stone walls are beautiful, long-lasting structures that are surprisingly easy to build provided you plan carefully. A low stone wall can be constructed without mortar using a centuries-old method known as dry-laying. With this technique, the wall is actually formed by two separate stacks that lean together slightly. The position and weight of the two stacks support each other, forming a single, sturdy wall. A dry-stone wall can be built to any length, but its width must be at least half of its height.

You can purchase stone for this project from a quarry or stone supplier, where different sizes, shapes, and colors of stone are sold, priced by the ton. The quarry or stone center can also sell you Type M mortar—necessary for bonding the capstones to the top of the wall.

Building dry-stone walls requires patience and a fair amount of physical effort. The stones must be sorted by size and shape. You'll probably also need to shape some of the stones to achieve consistent spacing and a general appearance that appeals to you.

To shape a stone, score it using a circular saw outfitted with a masonry blade. Place a mason's chisel on the score line and strike with a maul until the stone breaks. Wear safety glasses when using stonecutting tools.

It is easiest to build a dry-stone wall with ashlar—stone that has been split into roughly rectangular blocks. Ashlar stone is stacked in the same running-bond pattern used in brick wall construction; each stone overlaps a joint in the previous course. This technique avoids long vertical joints, resulting in a wall that is attractive and also strong.

How to Build a Dry-Stone Wall

Lay out the wall site using stakes and mason's string. Dig a 6"-deep trench that extends 6" beyond the wall on all sides. Add a 4" crushed stone sub-base to the trench, creating a "V" shape by sloping the sub-base so the center is about 2" deeper than the edges.

Select appropriate stones and lay the first course. Place pairs of stones side by side, flush with the edges of the trench and sloping toward the center. Use stones of similar height; position uneven sides face down. Fill any gaps between the shaping stones with small filler stones.

Lay the next course, staggering the joints. Use pairs of stones of varying lengths to offset the center joint. Alternate stone length and keep the height even, stacking pairs of thin stones if necessary to maintain consistent height. Place filler stones in the gaps.

Tie stones

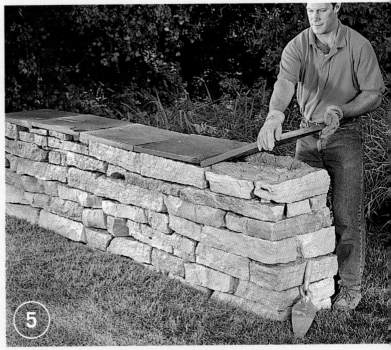

Every other course, place a tie stone every 3 ft. You may need to split the tie stones to length. Check the wall periodically for level.

Mortar the capstones to the top of the wall, keeping the mortar at least 6" from the edges so it's not visible. Push the capstones together and mortar the cracks in between. Brush off dried excess mortar with a stiff-bristle brush.

Mortared Garden Wall

TOOLS & MATERIALS

Tape measure	Garden hose
Pencil	Concrete materials
Chalk line	for foundation
Small whisk broom	Ashlar stone
Tools for mixing mortar	Type N or Type S mortar
Maul	Stakes and mason's line
Stone chisel	Scrap wood
Pitching chisel	Muriatic acid
Trowel	Bucket of water
Jointing tool	Sponge
Line level	Eye protection
Sponge	and work gloves

The mortared stone wall is a classic that brings structure and appeal to any yard or garden. Square-hewn ashlar and bluestone are the easiest to build with, though fieldstone and rubble also work well and make attractive walls.

Because the mortar turns the wall into a monolithic structure that can crack and heave with a freeze-thaw cycle, a concrete footing is required for a mortared stone wall. To maintain strength in the wall, use the heaviest, thickest stones for the base of the wall and thinner, flatter stones for the cap.

As you plan the wall layout, install tie stones—stones that span the width of the wall (page 127)—about every 3 feet, staggered through the courses both vertically and horizontally throughout the wall. Use the squarest, flattest stones to build the "leads," or ends of the wall

first, and then fill the middle courses. Plan for joints around 1 inch thick and make sure joints in successive courses do not line up. Follow this rule of thumb: cover joints below with a full stone above; locate joints above over a full stone below.

Laying a mortared stone wall is labor-intensive but satisfying work. Make sure to work safely and enlist friends to help with the heavy lifting.

A mortared stone wall made from ashlar adds structure and classic appeal to your home landscape. Plan carefully and enlist help to ease the building process.

How to Build a Mortared Stone Wall

Pour a footing for the wall and allow it to cure for 1 week. Measure and mark the wall location so it is centered on the footing. Snap chalk lines along the length of the footing for both the front and the back faces of the wall. Lay out corners using the 3-4-5 right angle method (see page 140).

Dry-lay the entire first course. Starting with a tie stone at each end, arrange stones in two rows along the chalk lines with joints about 1" thick. Use smaller stones to fill the center of the wall. Use larger, heavier stones in the base and lower courses. Place additional tie stones approximately every 3 ft. Trim stones as needed.

Mix a stiff batch of Type N or Type S mortar, following the manufacturer's directions. Starting at an end or corner, set aside some of the stone and brush off the foundation. Spread an even, 2" thick layer of mortar onto the foundation, about ½" from the chalk lines—the mortar will squeeze out a little.

Firmly press the first tie stone into the mortar so it is aligned with the chalk lines and relatively level. Tap the top of the stone with the handle of the trowel to set it. Continue to lay stones along each chalk line, working to the opposite end of the wall.

(continued)

VARIATION: You can also tool joints for a cleaner, tighter mortared joint. Tool joints when your thumb can leave an imprint in the mortar without removing any of it.

(5) **After installing the entire first course,** fill voids along the center of the wall that are larger than 2" with smaller rubble. Fill the remaining spaces and joints with mortar, using the trowel.

(6) **As you work, rake the joints** using a scrap of wood to a depth of ½"; raking joints highlights the stones rather than the mortared joints. After raking, use a whisk broom to even the mortar in the joints.

If heavy stones push out too much mortar, use wood wedges cut from scrap to hold the stone in place. Once the mortar sets up, remove the wedges and fill the voids with fresh mortar.

(7) **Drive stakes at the each end of the wall** and align a mason's line with the face of the wall. Use a line level to level the string at the height of the next course. Build up each end of the wall, called the "leads," making sure to stagger the joints between courses. Check the leads with a 4-ft. level on each wall face to make sure it is plumb.

Have a bucket of water and a sponge handy in case mortar oozes or spills onto the face of the stone. Wipe mortar away immediately before it can harden.

Install capstones by pressing flat stones that span the width of the wall into a mortar bed. Do not rake the joints, but clean off excess mortar with the trowel and clean excess mortar from the surface of the stones using a damp sponge.

9

Fill the middle courses between the leads by first dry-laying stones for placement and then mortaring them in place. Install tie stones about every 3 ft., both vertically and horizontally, staggering their position in each course. Make sure joints in successive courses do not fall in alignment.

11

Allow the wall to cure for one week and then clean it using a solution of 1 part muriatic acid and 10 parts water. Wet the wall using a garden hose, apply the acid solution, and then immediately rinse with plenty of clean, clear water. Always wear goggles, long sleeves and pants, and heavy rubber gloves when using acids.

Repairing Stone Walls

Damage to stonework is typically caused by frost heave, erosion or deterioration of mortar, or by stones that have worked out of place. Dry-stone walls are more susceptible to erosion and popping while mortared walls develop cracks that admit water, which can freeze and cause further damage.

Inspect stone structures once a year for signs of damage and deterioration. Replacing a stone or repointing crumbling mortar now will save you work in the long run.

A leaning stone column or wall probably suffers from erosion or foundation problems and can be dangerous if neglected. If you have the time, you can tear down and rebuild dry-laid structures, but mortared structures with excessive lean need professional help.

Stones in a wall can become dislodged due to soil settling, erosion, or seasonal freeze-thaw cycles. Make the necessary repairs before the problem migrates to other areas.

TOOLS & MATERIALS

Maul	Batter gauge	Masonry chisels	Replacement stones
Chisel	Stiff-bristle brush	Wood shims	Type M mortar
Camera	Trowels for mixing	Carpet-covered 2 × 4	Mortar tint
Shovel	and pointing	Chalk	Eye protection
Hand tamper	Mortar bag	Compactable gravel	Work gloves
Level			

REPAIRING POPPED STONES

Return a popped stone to its original position. If other stones have settled in its place, drive shims between neighboring stones to make room for the popped stone. Be careful not to wedge too far.

Use a 2 × 4 covered with carpet to avoid damaging the stone when hammering it into place. After hammering, make sure a replacement stone hasn't damaged or dislodged the adjoining stones.

How to Rebuild a Dry-Stone Wall Section

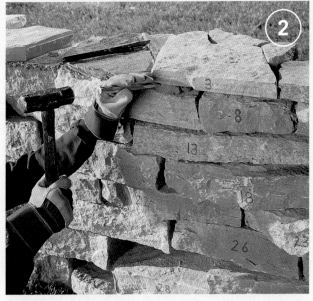

Study the wall and determine how much of it needs to be rebuilt. Plan to dismantle the wall in a V shape, centered on the damaged section. Number each stone and mark its orientation with chalk so you can rebuild it following the original design.

TIP: Photograph the wall, making sure the markings are visible.

Capstones are often set in a mortar bed atop the last course of stone. You may need to chip out the mortar with a maul and chisel to remove the capstones. Remove the marked stones, taking care to check the overall stability of the wall as you work.

EROSION

Rebuild the wall, one course at a time, using replacement stones only when necessary. Start each course at the ends and work toward the center. On thick walls, set the face stones first, and then fill in the center with smaller stones. Check your work with a level and use a batter gauge to maintain the batter of the wall. If your capstones were mortared, re-lay them in fresh mortar. Wash off the chalk with water and a stiff-bristle brush.

If you're rebuilding because of erosion, dig a trench at least 6" deep under the damaged area, and fill it with compactable gravel. Tamp the gravel with a hand tamper. This will improve drainage and prevent water from washing soil out from beneath the wall.

Tips for Repairing Mortared Stone Walls

Tint mortar for repair work so it blends with the existing mortar. Mix several samples of mortar, adding a different amount of tint to each and allow them to dry thoroughly. Compare each sample to the old mortar and choose the closest match.

Use a mortar bag to restore weathered and damaged mortar joints over an entire structure. Remove loose mortar (see below) and clean all surfaces with a stiff-bristle brush and water. Dampen the joints before tuck-pointing and cover all of the joints, smoothing and brushing as necessary.

How to Repoint Mortar Joints

Carefully rake out cracked and crumbling mortar, stopping when you reach solid mortar. Remove loose mortar and debris with a stiff-bristle brush.

TIP: Rake the joints with a chisel and maul or make your own raking tool by placing an old screwdriver in a vise and bending the shaft about 45°.

(1)

(2)

Mix Type M mortar, and then dampen the repair surfaces with clean water. Working from the top down, pack mortar into the crevices using a pointing trowel. Smooth the mortar when it has set up enough to resist light finger pressure. Remove excess mortar with a stiff-bristle brush.

How to Replace a Mortared Stone Wall

Remove the damaged stone by chiseling out the surrounding mortar using a masonry chisel or a modified screwdriver (opposite page). Drive the chisel toward the damaged stone to avoid harming neighboring stones. Once the stone is out, chisel the surfaces inside the cavity as smooth as possible.

Brush out the cavity to remove loose mortar and debris. Test the surrounding mortar and chisel or scrape out any mortar that isn't firmly bonded.

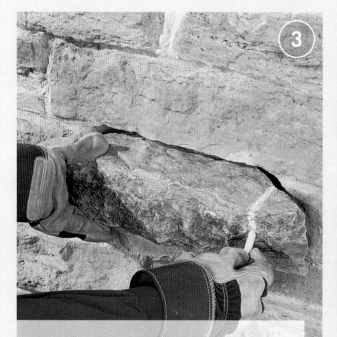

Dry-fit the replacement stone. The stone should be stable in the cavity and blend with the rest of the wall. You can mark the stone with chalk and cut it to fit, but excessive cutting will result in a conspicuous repair.

Mist the stone and cavity lightly, and then apply Type M mortar around the inside of the cavity using a trowel. Butter all mating sides of the replacement stone. Insert the stone and wiggle it forcefully to remove any air pockets. Use a pointing trowel to pack the mortar solidly around the stone. Smooth the mortar when it has set up.

Fences

It has been said that good fences make good neighbors. If this is true, it would seem that good fences are a must in your neighborhood, right? So the key question is: what makes good fences?

The answer: this chapter.

It's not easy to find a property that doesn't have fencing, and there are several reasons why this is so:

- People are proud to define their property line, and fences provide definition.
- Homeowners often desire the privacy that fences offer.
- Fencing blocks an unattractive view and establishes a frame that showcases your picture-book yard.
- In some cases, fences create boundaries against unwanted deer, dogs, and other four-legged critters that might wander into your yard.
- Fences themselves show design character and style that make them a focal point.
- Fences highlight the slope and flow of your land. A hill crowned with a fence creates natural angles that attract the eye.

Perhaps the most compelling reason that fences are so prevalent? They're doable. You can build a fence—it's not tricky work—and as you do, you can enjoy the outdoors and accomplish a straightforward project at your own pace. It's hugely satisfying work that in short order transforms your property.

In This Chapter:
- Designing Fences: Slope
- Setting Posts
- Picket Fence
- Post & Board Fence
- Split Rail Fence
- Wood Composite Fence
- Vinyl Panel Fence
- Ornamental Metal Fence
- Bamboo Fence

Designing Fences: Slope

It's considerably easier to build a fence when the ground is flat and level along the entire length of the proposed site line. But few landscapes are entirely flat. Hills, slight valleys, or consistent downward grades are slope issues to resolve while planning your fence. There are two common ways to handle slope: contouring and stepping.

With a contoured fence, the stringers are parallel to the ground, while the posts and siding are plumb to the earth. The top of the fence maintains a consistent height above grade, following the contours of the land. Most pre-assembled panel fences cannot be contoured, since the vertical siding members are set square to the stringers. Picket fence panels may be "racked" out of square for gentle contouring. Vinyl fence sections generally permit contouring.

Each section of a stepped fence is level across the top, forming the characteristic steps as the ground rises or falls. Stepped fences appear more structured and formal. Pre-assembled panels may be stepped to the degree their bottoms can be trimmed for the slope or that additional siding (such as kick boards) can be added to conceal gaps at the tall end of the step. Stepped custom-built fences are more work than contoured fences since vertical siding boards must be trimmed to length individually and post heights may vary within a layout.

Solid planning and careful execution allow you to turn a sloped yard into a positive design factor when you build your fence or wall project.

Strategies for Managing Slope

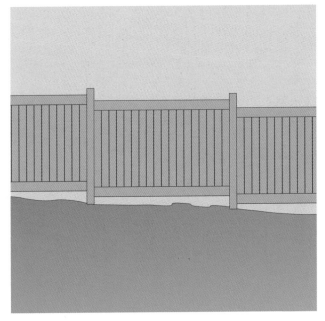

Stepped panels are horizontal, maintaining an even height between posts. A good strategy for pre-built panel systems, stepping fences is the only way to handle slope when working with panels that cannot be trimmed, racked, or otherwise altered.

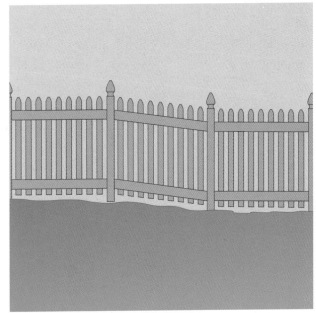

Racking a panel involves manipulating a simple fence panel by twisting it out of square so the stringers follow a low slope while the siding remains vertical. Stockade and picket panels are good candidates for this trick, but the degree to which you can rack the panels is limited. If the siding is connected to stringers with more than one fastener at each joint, you'll need to remove some fasteners and replace them after racking the panel.

Contouring creates a more casual, natural-looking fence. Each individual siding board is set the same distance from the ground below and allowed to extend to full height without trimming. The resulting top of the fence will mimic the ground contour.

Bottom trimming creates a level fenceline with a baseline that follows the slope and contour of the land. On low slopes you can use this technique and trim the siding boards on pre-made panels that have open bottoms (in some cases you can raise the bottom stringer). Bottom trimming is best for site-built board and stringer fences, however.

Contoured Fences

A contoured fence rolls along with the terrain, maintaining a consistent height above the ground as it follows the land. Picket fences and others with individual siding work best for contouring. There are multiple tactics you can use to build a contoured fence. The scenario described below involves setting all your posts, installing stringers, trimming posts to uniform height above the top stringer and then adding the picket siding.

Contoured installation overview. Begin the layout by running a string between batter boards or stakes located at the ends and corners of the fenceline, adding intermediate batter boards or stakes as needed to keep the string roughly parallel with the grade. Mark the post centers at regular distances (usually 6 or 8 feet) on the string. Don't forget to allow for the posts when measuring. Drop a plumb bob at each post mark on the string to determine posthole locations. Mark these locations with a piece of plastic pegged to the ground or by another method of your choosing.

Align, space, and set the posts (if appropriate for your fence type). Attach the lower stringers between posts. If you are using metal fence rail brackets, bend the lower tab on each bracket to match the slope of the stringer. Each stringer should follow the slope of the ground below as closely as possible while maintaining a minimum distance between the highest point of the ground and the bottom of the stringer. This distance will vary from fence to fence according to your design, but 12 inches is a good general rule.

Install all of the lower stringers and then install the upper stringers parallel to the lower ones. Make sure to maintain an even spacing between the stringers. Establish the distance from the upper stringer to the post tops and then measure this distance on each post. Draw cutting lines and trim the post tops using a circular saw and a speed square clamped to the post as a guide.

Make a spacer that's about the same width as the siding boards, with a height that matches the planned distance from the ground to the bottom of each siding board. Set the spacer beneath each board as you install it. You'll also want a spacer to set the gap between siding boards. Install the siding and add post caps.

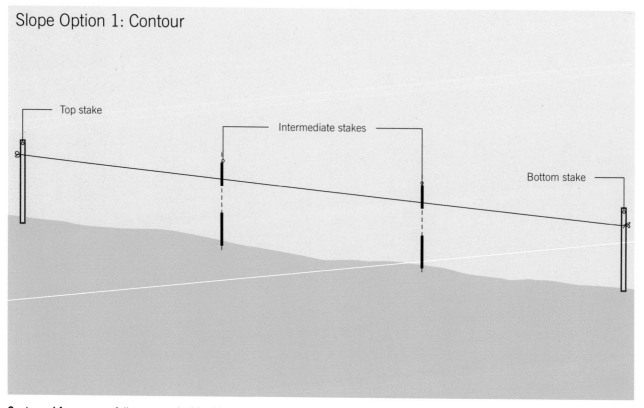

Slope Option 1: Contour

Top stake

Intermediate stakes

Bottom stake

Contoured fences can follow ground with either a regular slope or an irregular slope. Place a stake at the beginning and end of the fence line and at each corner. Add intermediate stakes to maintain spacing when the slope changes.

Stepped Fences

A stepped fence retains its shape and configuration regardless of changes in slope. The effect of the stepping up or down of whole panels it to create a more formal appearance, but it also lets you avoid cutting premade fence panels. The sacrifice is that you often end up with very tall fence posts and you may need to add filler wood between panel bottoms and irregular dips in the ground.

The following stepping technique works over slopes of a consistent grade. If the grade changes much, bracket each new slope with its own stake or pair of batter boards, as in the illustration on the previous page. Treat the last post of the first run as the first post of the second run and so on.

Alternatively, step each section independently, trimming the post tops after the siding is set. The scenario below describes a flat cap stringer, which some fences use to create a smooth top. If this is not needed on your fence, simply measure down the appropriate distances to position the inset or face-mounted stringers.

Stepped installation overview. Using mason's string and stakes or batter boards, establish a level line that follows the fence line. Measure the length of the string from end stake to end stake. This number is the run. Divide the run into equal segments that are between 72 and 96 inches. This will give you the number of sections and posts (number of sections plus one).

Measure from the ground to the string at both end stakes. The difference between the two measurements is the rise of the slope. Divide the rise by the number of fence sections on the slope to find the stepping measurement.

Measure and mark the post locations along the level string with permanent marker "Vs" on tape. Drop a plumb bob from each post location mark on the string. Mark the ground with a nail and a piece of bright plastic.

Set the first post at one end and the next one in line. Mark the trim line for cutting to height and run a level string from the cutting line to the next post. Measure up (or down) from the string for the step size distance. Adjust marks if necessary before cutting the posts.

Repeat until you reach the end of the fence line. Avoid creating sections that will be too tall or too short. The bottom stringer should remain at least 4 inches above grade.

Cut all posts and then attach stringers or panels so the distance from the tops of the posts to the stringers is consistent.

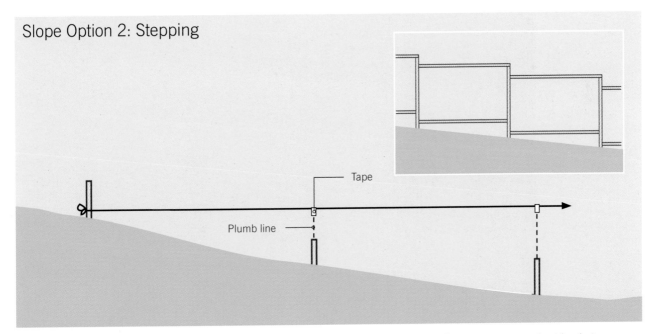

Slope Option 2: Stepping

Tape

Plumb line

Stepped fences (inset) can be installed on either regular or irregular slopes. To plan the fence, run a mason's string between stakes or batter boards at the high end and the low end of the fence line; measure the distance from the string to the ground at both ends, then calculate the difference between measurements to find the total rise. Divide this amount by the number of fence sections to determine the stepping measurement for each fence panel. On irregular slopes, the amount of drop will vary from section to section.

Laying Out Fence Lines

Fence installations begin with plotting the fence line and marking post locations. Make a site map and carefully measure each post location. The more exact the posthole positions, the less likely it is that you'll need to cut stringers and siding to special sizes.

For walls, determine the outside edges of the footings along the entire site, as for a fence line. Then plot right angles to find the ends and inside edges of the footings.

Laying out a fence or wall with square corners or curves involves a little more work than for a straight fence line. The key for these techniques is the same as for plotting a straight fenceline: measure and mark accurately. This will ensure proper spacing between the posts and accurate dimensions for footings, which will provide strength and support for each structure.

How to lay out a straight fence line. Determine your exact property lines. Plan your fence line with the locally required setback (usually 6 to 12 inches) from the property line, unless you and your neighbor have come to another agreement. Draw a site map. It should take all aspects of your landscape into consideration, with the location of each post marked. Referring to the site map, mark the fence line with stakes at each end or corner-post location.

Drive a pair of wood stakes a couple of feet beyond each corner or end stake. Screw a level crossboard across the stakes about 6 inches up from the ground on the highest end of the fence run. Draw a mason's string from the first batter board down the fence line. Level the line with a line level and mark the height of the line against one stake of the second batter board pair. Attach a level batter board to these stakes at this height and tie the string to the crossboard so it is taut.

To mark gates, first find the on-center spacing for the gateposts. Combine the width of the gate, the clearance necessary for the hinges and latch hardware, and the actual width of one post. Mark the string with a "V" of masking tape to indicate the center point of each gatepost.

To mark remaining posts, refer to your site map, and then measure and mark the line post locations on the string with marks on masking tape. Remember that the marks indicate the center of the posts, not the edges.

Use a pair of wood stakes and mason's string to plot the rough location of your fence or wall. Then, for greater accuracy, install batter boards to plot the final location.

Tips for Installing Batter Board

To install batter boards, drive a pair of short wood stakes a couple of feet beyond each corner or end of the rough planned fenceline. Screw a level crossboard across one pair of stakes, about 6" up from the ground on the higher end of the fence run. Loosely tie a mason's string to the middle of the crossboard.

First pair of stakes

Crossboard

Second pair of stakes

Line from first pair of stakes

Stretch the mason's line from the batter board to the second pair of stakes at the opposite end or corner of the run. Draw the string tight and level it with a line level. Mark the string's position onto one of the stakes. Fasten a crossboard to the second pair of stakes so it is level and its top is aligned with the mark on the stake. Tie the mason's line to the center of the crossboard.

Measure out from the starting points of the fence line and mark post locations directly onto the layout lines using pieces of masking tape (don't forget to allow for the widths of your posts—see tips below).

Post location

TIPS FOR SPACING LINE POSTS AND GATEPOSTS

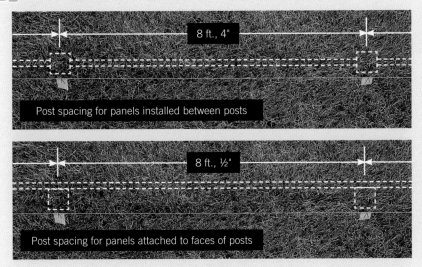

8 ft., 4"

Post spacing for panels installed between posts

8 ft., ½"

Post spacing for panels attached to faces of posts

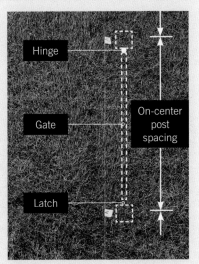

Hinge

Gate

Latch

On-center post spacing

If your fence panels will be installed between fence posts (top photo) and you are using 4 × 4 wood posts, add 4" to the length of the fence panels and use that distance as the on-center span between posts (the 4 × 4 posts are actually only 3½" wide but the extra ½" created by using the full 4" dimension will create just the right amount of "wiggle room" for the panel). If panels will be attached to the post faces, add ½" to the actual panel width to determine post spacing.

To find the on-center spacing of gateposts, add the gate width, the clearance needed for hinge and gate hardware, and the actual diameter of one post.

Laying Out Right Angles

If your fence or wall will enclose a square or rectangular area, or if it joins a building, you probably want the corners to form 90-degree angles. There are many techniques for establishing a right angle when laying out an outdoor project, but the 3-4-5-triangle method is the easiest and most reliable. It is a simple method of squaring your fence layout lines, but if you have the space use a 6-8-10 or 9-12-15 triangle. Whichever dimensions you choose, you'll find it easier to work with two tape measures to create the triangle.

How to Lay Out a Right Angle

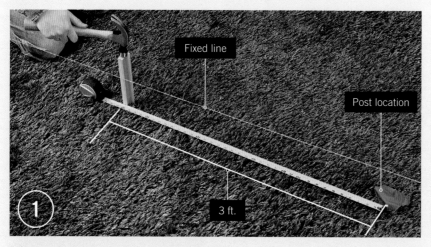

Drive a pair of stakes along a known fence line and run a line that crosses the corner post location (this line should stay fixed as a reference while you square the crossing line to it). Drive a stake 3 ft. out from the corner post location, on the line you don't want to move. You will adjust the other line to establish the right angle.

Draw one tape measure from the post location roughly at a right angle to the fixed line. Draw the tape beyond the 4 ft. mark and lock it.

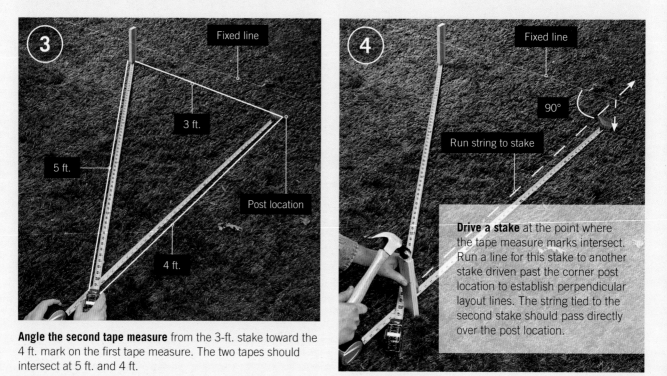

Angle the second tape measure from the 3-ft. stake toward the 4 ft. mark on the first tape measure. The two tapes should intersect at 5 ft. and 4 ft.

Drive a stake at the point where the tape measure marks intersect. Run a line for this stake to another stake driven past the corner post location to establish perpendicular layout lines. The string tied to the second stake should pass directly over the post location.

Laying Out Curves

A curve in a fenceline or wall must be laid out evenly for quality results. One easy way to accomplish this is to make a crude compass by tying one end of a string around a can of marking paint and tying the other end to a wood stake, as shown in Step 3 below. The radius of the curve should equal the distance from the compass' pivot stake to the starting points of the curve, so make sure to tie the string to this length.

How to Lay Out a Curve

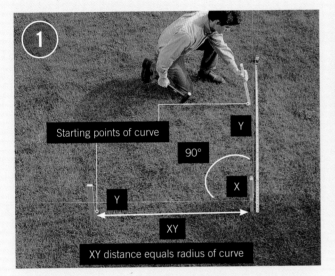

Plot a right angle at the corner of the outline, using the 3-4-5 method (see page 140). Measure and drive stakes equidistant from the outside corner to mark the starting points for the curve (labeled "Y" here).

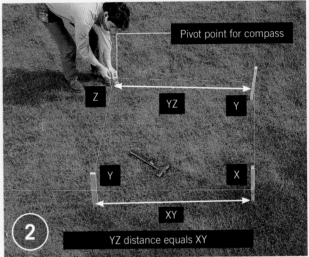

Tie a mason's string to each Y stake, and extend the strings back to the corner stake. Hold the strings tight at the point where they meet. Then, pull the strings outward at the meeting point until they are taut. Drive a stake at this point to create a perfect square. This stake (labeled "Z" here) will be the pivot point for your string compass.

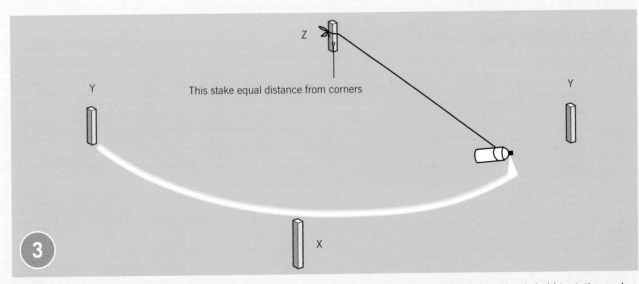

Mark the curve: Tie a mason's string to the pivot point (Z) and to a can of marking paint. When the string is held taut, the can's spray nozzle should be even with the stakes at the start of the curve (Y). Keeping the string taut, spray the ground in a smooth arc, extending the curve between the two Y stakes.

Setting Posts

Taking the time to make sure posts are vertical and positioned precisely is perhaps the most important aspect of a successful fence building project.

Even among professional landscapers you'll find widely differing practices for setting fence posts. Some take the always-overbuild approach and set every post in concrete that extends a foot past the frostline. Others prefer the impermanence, adjustability, and drainage of setting posts in packed sand or gravel. Some treat the post ends before setting the posts, others don't bother. The posts may be set all at once, prior to installing the stringers and siding; or, they may be set one at a time in a build-as-you-go approach. Before deciding which approach is best for your situation, it's a good idea to simply walk around your neighborhood and see how the posts for similar fences are installed, then assess which posts seem to be holding up the best.

Another area of dispute is at which point in the process posts should be cut to length (height). While there are those who advocate cutting all posts before installation and then aligning them in the ground before setting them (especially when installing chain link), the most reliable method is to trim the posts to height with a circular saw or handsaw after they are set in the ground and the concrete has set.

Here are some additional thoughts to help you decide how to set your posts:

- Tamped earth and gravel post setting have been increasing the life span and stability of posts for thousands of years by keeping the immediate surroundings of the post drier and firmer.
- The shallow, dish-shaped concrete footing breaks all the rules, but is often the only footing that works in very loose sandy soils. Check with local fence contractors to make sure it's right for your area.
- Common posts are set high enough to be trimmed down to their final height. Posts with pre-cut mortises (such as split rail fence posts) or finials need to be set to the final height in the hole.
- Dig holes two times the post thickness for sand-set or gravel-set and closer to three times the diameter if concrete-set.
- For long-term strength, set all gateposts and end posts in concrete.

The most reliably long-lasting wood posts are pressure-treated with chemicals and labeled for ground contact. Species that are naturally rot resistant are unfortunately less so today than in yesteryear.

Once you've plotted your fenceline with batter boards and string, mark and dig the postholes. Remove the string for digging, but leave the batter boards in place; you will need these for aligning the posts when you set them.

As a general rule, posts should be buried at a minimum depth equal to ⅓ of the total post length (e.g., a post for a 6-foot-tall fence will be approximately 9 feet long, with 3 feet buried in the ground). Check with your city's building department for the post depth and burial method required by the local building code. Posts set in concrete should always extend below the frost line.

TOOLS & MATERIALS

Plumb bob	Masking tape
Hand maul	Tape measure
Posthole digger	Speed square
Shovel	Colored plastic
Coarse gravel	Nails
Carpenter's level	Eye and ear protection
Concrete	Drill/driver
Mason's trowel	Screws
4 × 4 posts	Circular saw
Scrap lengths of 2 × 4	Clamps
Mason's string	Work gloves
Post level	

How to Set Fence Posts

Set batter boards at both ends of the fence line. String a mason's line between the batter boards and level it. Mark post locations on the string with masking tape according to your plan.

Transfer the marks from the string to the ground, using a plumb bob to pinpoint the post locations. Pin a piece of colored plastic to the ground with a nail at each post location.

Depth gauge

30"

Dig postholes using a clamshell-type posthole digger (left photo) or a rented power auger (right photo). Posthole diggers work well for most situations, but if your holes are deeper than 30", you'll need to widen the hole at the top to operate the digger, so consider using a power auger. Make a depth gauge by tacking a board onto a 2 × 4 at the hole depth from the end of the 2 × 4. As you dig, check the depth with the gauge. If you'll be filling the posthole with concrete, widen the bottoms of the holes with your posthole digger to create bell shapes. This is especially important in locales where the ground freezes.

(continued)

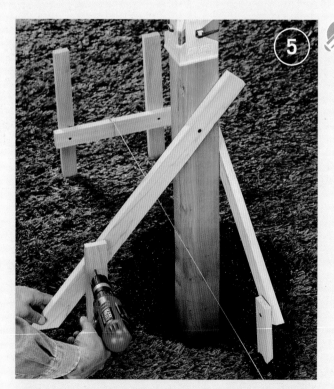

Reset the mason's string as a guide for aligning posts. If you want the post to be in exactly the same spot it was laid out, shift the string half the thickness of the post. Pour a 6" layer of gravel into each hole for improved drainage. Position each post in its hole.

Original position of line

TUBULAR FORMS

For full concrete footings in frost-heave-prone soils, cut 8"-dia. concrete forming tubes into 18" sections to collar the posts near grade level and prevent the concrete from spreading. Holes tend to flare at the top, giving concrete footings a lip that freezing ground can push against.

MIXING CONCRETE

Align your post along one line (or two if it's a corner post). Brace the post on adjacent sides with boards screwed to wood stakes. Adjust to plumb in both directions, anchoring each brace to the post with screws when plumb. As you plumb the post, keep the post flush against the line. Set the remaining posts the same way.

If you've never filled postholes with concrete before, you will be amazed at how much it takes to fill a hole. A 12"-dia. hole that's 36" deep will require around 3 cubic feet of concrete—or, about six 60-lb. bags of dry mix. If you're installing 10 posts, that's 60 bags. This is yet another reason why setting posts one at a time is a good idea—you can spread out the heavy labor of mixing concrete in a wheelbarrow or mortar tub. If you'll be needing more than 1 cubic yard (27 cubic feet), consider having ready-mix concrete trucked in. But make sure all your posts are braced and set and have at least two wheelbarrows and three workers on hand.

(6)

Mix concrete in a wheelbarrow and tamp into the hole with a 2 × 4 to pack the concrete as tightly as you can. Recheck the post alignment and plumb as you go, while correction is still possible.

TIP: Mask the post with waxed paper near the collaring point of the concrete to keep the visible portion of the post clean. Remove the waxed paper before the concrete sets up.

Form a rounded crown of concrete with your trowel just above grade to shed water.

(7)

For reasonably level ground, draw a mason's string from end post to end post at the height the posts need to be cut (for custom fences, this height might be determined by your shortest post). Mark each post at the string. Carry the line around each post with a pencil and speed square.

(8)

Wait at least a day for the concrete to set up and then clamp a cutting guide to the posts (a speed square is perfect). Cut along the trim line on each face of each with a circular saw to trim your posts (this is a great time to use a cordless circular saw). In most cases, you'll want to add a post cap later to cover the end grain.

Picket Fence

TOOLS & MATERIALS

Tools and materials for setting posts	
Mason's string	Galvanized or stainless-steel finish nails
Line level	Spacer
Circular saw	Speed square
Drill	Eye and ear protection
Power miter saw	Clamps
Sander	Paint brush
2-ft. level	Tape measure
Lumber (4 × 4, 2 × 4, 1 × 4)	16d galvanized common nails
Deck screws (3½", 2")	Wood sealant or primer
Finishing materials	Work gloves
Post caps (optional)	Pencil
Hammer	Finish materials

The quintessential symbol of American hominess, the classic picket fence remains a perennial favorite for more than its charm and good looks. It's also a deceptively effective boundary, creating a clear line of separation while appearing to be nothing more than a familiar decoration. This unique characteristic of a welcoming barrier makes the picket fence a good choice for enclosing an area in front of the house. It's also a popular option for separating a vegetable or flower garden from the surrounding landscape.

Building a custom picket fence from scratch is a great do-it-yourself project. The small scale and simple structure of the basic fence design make it easy to add your own creative details and personal touches. In this project, you'll see how to cut custom pickets and build a fence using standard lumber (plus an easy upgrade of adding decorative post caps). As an alternative, you can build your fence using prefab fence panels for the picket infill. You can also buy pre-cut pickets at home centers, lumberyards, and online retailers to save on the work of cutting your own.

Traditionally, a picket fence is about 3 to 4 feet tall (if taller than 4 feet, a picket fence starts to look like a barricade) with 1 × 3 or 1 × 4 pickets. Fence posts can be spaced anywhere up to 8 feet apart if you're using standard lightweight pickets. Depending on your preference, the posts can be visible design elements or they can hide behind a continuous line of pickets. Spacing between the pickets is a question of function and taste: go with whatever spacing looks best and fulfills your functional needs.

A low picket fence adds curb appeal and a cozy sense of enclosure to a front yard or entry area without blocking views to or from the house.

Picket Fence Styles

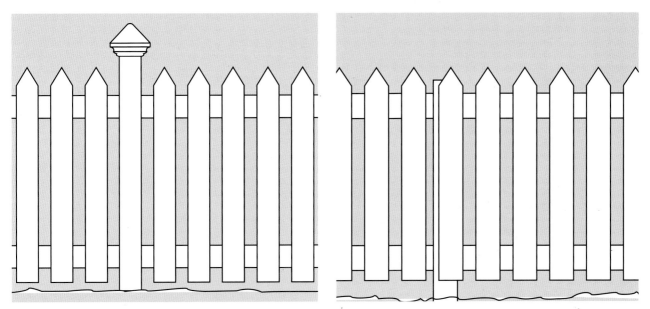

Highlighting the posts (left) gives the fence a sectional look, and the rhythm of the pickets is punctuated by the slower cadence of the posts. To create this effect, mount the stringers on edge, so the pickets are flush with—or recessed from—the front faces of the posts. Hiding the posts (right) creates an unbroken line of pickets and a somewhat less structural look overall. This effect calls for stringers installed flush with—or over the front of—the post faces.

How to Build a Picket Fence

Install and trim the posts according to your plan. In this project, the pickets stand at 36" above grade, and the posts are 38" (without the post caps). Set the posts in concrete, and space them as desired—but no more than 96" on center.

Mark the stringer positions onto the posts. Measure down from each post top and make marks at 8" and 28½" (or as desired for your design). These marks represent the top edges of the two stringer boards for each fence section. *(continued)*

3

Install the stringers. Measure between each pair of posts, and cut the 2 × 4 stringers to fit. Drill angled pilot holes and fasten the stringers to the posts with 3½" deck screws or 16d galvanized common nails; drive one fastener in the bottom and top edges of each stringer end.

CALCULATING PICKET SPACING

Determine the picket quantity and spacing. Cut a few pickets (Steps 5 to 7) and experiment with different spacing to find the desired (approximate) gap between pickets. Calculate the precise gap dimension and number of pickets needed for each section using the formula shown in the example here.

Total space between posts: 92.5"

Unit size (picket width + approx. gap size):
3.5" + 1.75" = 5.25"

Number of pickets (post space ÷ unit size):
92.5" ÷ 5.25" = 17. 62 (round down for slightly larger gaps; round up for slightly smaller gaps)

Total picket area (# of pickets × picket width):
17 × 3.5" = 59.5"

Remaining space for gaps (post space - total picket area): 92.5" - 59.5" = 33"

Individual gap size (total gap space ÷ [# of pickets + 1]): 33" ÷ 18 = 1.83"

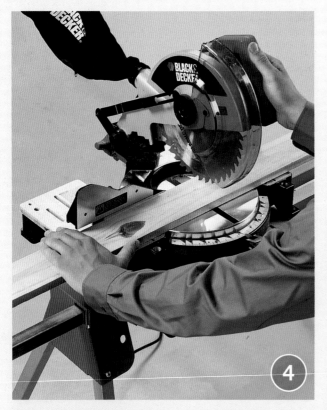

4

Cut the pickets to length using a power miter saw. To save time, set up a stop block with the distance from the block to blade equal to the picket length.

TIP: If you're painting the fence, you can save money by cutting the pickets from 12-ft.-long boards of pressure-treated lumber. In this project, the pickets are 32" long; each board yields four pickets.

Shape the picket ends as desired. For straight-cut designs, use a miter saw with a stop block on the right side of the blade (the first pass cuts through the picket and the block). If the shape is symmetrical, such as this 90° point, cut off one corner, and then flip the board over and make the second cut—no measuring or adjusting is needed.

5

VARIATION: To cut pickets with decorative custom shapes, create a cardboard or hardboard template with the desired shape. Trace the shape onto each picket and make the cuts. Use a jigsaw for curved cuts. Gang several cut pieces together for final shaping with a sander.

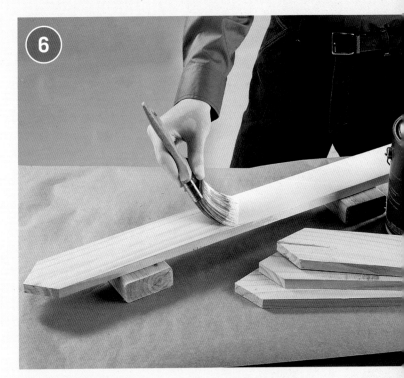

Prime or seal all surfaces of the posts, stringers, and pickets; and then add at least one coat of finish (paint, stain, or sealer), as desired. This will help protect even the unexposed surfaces from rot.

Set up a string line to guide the picket installation. Clamp a mason's string to two posts at the desired height for the tops of the pickets.

NOTE: To help prevent rot and to facilitate grass trimming, plan to install the pickets at least 2" above the ground.

Install the pickets. Using a cleat spacer cut to the width of the picket gap, set each picket in place and drill even pairs of pilot holes into each stringer. Fasten the pickets with 2" deck screws. Check the first picket (and every few thereafter) for plumb with a level before piloting.

Add the post caps. Wood post caps (with or without metal cladding) offer an easy way to dress up plain posts while protecting the end grain from water. Install caps with galvanized or stainless-steel finish nails, or as directed by the manufacturer. Apply the final finish coat or touch-ups to the entire fence.

Post & Board Fence

TOOLS & MATERIALS

Tools and materials for setting posts

Mason's string

Line level

Circular saw

Speed square

Clamps

Circular saw

Drill

4 × 4 posts

Finishing materials

Bar clamps

Chisel

Primer paint or stain

3" stainless-steel screws

Post levels

Combination square

Eye and ear protection

Lumber (1 × 6, 1 × 4, 2 × 6, 1 × 3)

Deck screws (2", 2½", 3½")

8d galvanized nails

Scrap 2 × 4

Work gloves

Pencil

Post and board fences include an endless variety of simple designs in which widely spaced square or round posts support several horizontal boards. This type of fence has been around since the early 1700s, when it began to be praised for its efficient use of lumber and land and its refined appearance. The post and board is still a great design today. Even in a contemporary suburban setting, a classic, white three- or four-board fence evokes the stately elegance of a horse farm or the welcoming, down-home feel of a farmhouse fence bordering a country lane.

Another desirable quality of post and board fencing is its ease in conforming to slopes and rolling ground. In fact, it often looks best when the fence rises and dips with ground contours. Of course, you can also build the fence so it's level across the top by trimming the posts along a level line. Traditional agricultural versions of post and board fences typically include three to five boards spaced evenly apart or as needed to contain livestock. If you like the look of widely spaced boards but need a more complete barrier for pets, cover the back side of the fence with galvanized wire fencing, which is relatively unnoticeable behind the bold lines of the fence boards. You can also use the basic post and board structure to create any number of custom designs. The fence styles shown in the following pages are just a sampling of what you can build using the basic construction technique for post and board fences.

A low post and board fence, like traditional picket fencing, is both decorative and functional, creating a modest enclosure without blocking views. The same basic fence made taller and with tighter board spacing becomes an attractive privacy screen or security fence.

How to Build a Classic Post & Board Fence

Set the posts in concrete, following the desired spacing (see page 148). Laying out the posts at 96" on center allows for efficient use of lumber. For smaller boards, such as 1 × 4s and smaller, set posts closer together for better rigidity.

Trim and shape the posts with a circular saw. For a contoured fence, measure up from the ground and mark the post height according to your plan (post height shown here is 36"). For a level fence, mark the post heights with a level string (see page 149). If desired, cut a 45° chamfer on the post tops using a speed square to ensure straight cuts. Prime and paint (or stain and seal) the posts.

Mark the board locations by measuring down from the top of each post and making a mark representing the top edge of each board. The traditional three-board design employs even spacing between boards. Use a speed square to draw a line across the front faces of the posts at each height mark. Mark the post centers on alternate posts using a combination square or speed square and pencil. For strength, it's best to stagger the boards so that butted end joints occur at every other post (this requires 16-ft. boards for posts set 8-ft. apart). The centerlines represent the location of each butted joint. *(continued)*

Install 1 × 6 boards. Measure and mark each board for length and then cut it to size. Clamp the board to the posts, following the height and center marks. Drill pilot holes and fasten each board end with three 2½" deck screws or 8d galvanized box nails. Use three fasteners where long boards pass over posts as well.

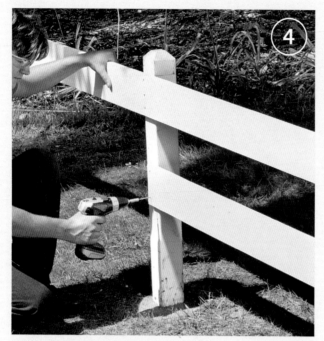

Mark for mitered butt joints at changes in elevation. To mark the miters on contoured fences, draw long centerlines onto the posts. Position an uncut board over the posts at the proper height and then mark where the top and bottom edges meet the centerline. Connect the marks to create the cutting line and make the cut.

NOTE: The mating board must have the same angle for a symmetrical joint.

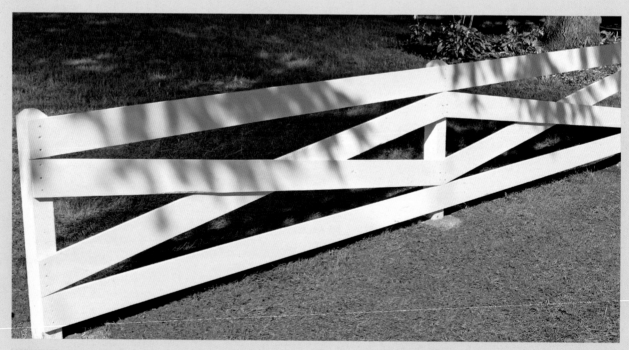

VARIATION: This charming fence style with crossed middle boards calls for a simple alteration of the classic three-board fence. To build this version, complete the installation of the posts and top and bottom boards, following the same techniques used for the classic fence.

TIP: If desired, space the posts closer together for steeper cross angles. Then, mark long centerlines on the posts and use them to mark the angled end cuts for the middle boards. When installed, the middle boards lap over each other, creating a slight bow in the center that adds interest to the overall look.

How to Build a Notched Post & Board Fence

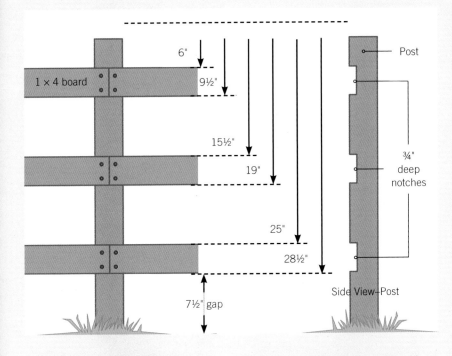

1 × 4 board

6"

9½"

15½"

19"

25"

28½"

7½" gap

Post

¾" deep notches

Side View—Post

The notched-post fence presents a slight variation on the standard face-mounted fence design. Here, each run of boards is let into a notch in the posts so the boards install flush with the post faces. This design offers a cleaner look and adds strength overall to the fence. In this example, the boards are 1 × 4s so the posts are set 6 ft. on center; 1 × 6 or 2 × 6 boards would allow for wider spacing (8 ft.).

NOTE: Because the notches must be precisely aligned between posts, the posts are set and braced before the concrete is added. Alternatively, you can complete the post installation and then mark the notches with a string and cut each one with the posts in place.

Cut and mark the posts. Cut the 4 × 4 posts to length at 66". Clamp the posts together with their ends aligned and mark the notches at 6", 9½", 15½", 19", 25", and 28½" down from the top ends.

Create the notches. Make a series of parallel cuts between the notch marks using a circular saw with the blade depth set at ¾". Clean out the waste and smooth the bases of the notches with a chisel.

Install the posts and boards. Set the posts in their holes and brace them in place using a level string to align the notches (see page 149). Secure the posts with concrete. Prefinish all fence parts. Install the 1 × 4 boards with 2" deck screws (driven through pilot holes) so their ends meet at the middle of each post.

How to Build a Capped Post & Board Fence

A cap rail adds a finished look to a low post and board fence. This fence design includes a 2 × 6 cap rail and an infill made of alternating 1 × 4 and 1 × 6 boards for a decorative pattern and a somewhat more enclosed feel than you get with a basic three-board fence. The cap pieces are mitered over the corner posts. Where cap boards are joined together over long runs of fence, they should meet at a scarf joint—made with opposing 30° or 45° bevels cut into the end of each board. All scarf and miter joints should occur over the center of a post.

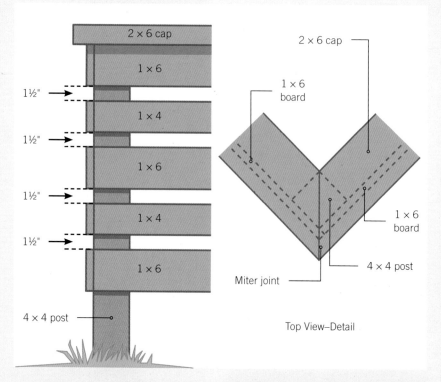

2 × 6 cap

1 × 6

1½"

1 × 4

1½"

1 × 6

1½"

1 × 4

1½"

1 × 6

4 × 4 post

2 × 6 cap

1 × 6 board

1 × 6 board

4 × 4 post

Miter joint

Top View—Detail

Install and mark the posts. Set the 4 × 4 posts in concrete with 72" on-center spacing. Trim the post tops so they are level with one another and approximately 36" above grade. Prefinish all fence parts. Use a square and pencil to mark a vertical centerline on each post where the board ends will butt together.

Install the boards. For each infill bay, cut two 1 × 4s and three 1 × 6s to length. Working from the top of the posts down, fasten the boards with 2½" deck screws driven through pilot holes. Use a 1½"-thick spacer (such as a 2 × 4 laid flat) to ensure even spacing between boards.

Add the cap rail. Cut the cap boards so they will install flush with the inside faces and corners of the posts; this creates a 1¼" overhang beyond the boards on the front side of the fence. Fasten the cap pieces to the posts with 3½" deck screws driven through pilot holes.

How to Build a Modern Post & Board Privacy Fence

This beautiful, modern-style post and board fence is made with pressure-treated 4 × 4 posts and clear cedar 1 × 3, 1 × 4, and 1 × 6 boards. To ensure quality and color consistency, it's a good idea to hand-pick the lumber, and choose S4S (surfaced on four sides) for a smooth, sleek look. Alternative materials include clear redwood, ipé, and other rot-resistant species. A high-quality, UV-resistant finish is critical to preserve the wood's natural coloring for as long as possible.

Install the posts, spacing them 60" on-center or as desired. Mark the tops of the posts with a level line, and trim them at 72" above grade.

NOTE: This fence design is best suited to level ground. Cut the fence boards to length. If desired, you can rip down wider stock for custom board widths (but you'll have to sand off any saw marks for a finished look).

Fasten the boards to the post faces using 2½" deck screws or 8d galvanized box nails driven through pilot holes. Work from the top down, and use ⅞"-thick wood spacers to ensure accurate spacing.

Add the battens to cover the board ends and hide the posts. Use 1 × 4 boards for the infill posts and 1 × 6s for the corner posts. Rip ¾" from the edge of one corner batten so the assembly is the same width on both sides. Fasten the battens to the posts with 3" stainless-steel screws (other screw materials can discolor the wood).

Split Rail Fence

The split rail, or post and rail, fence is essentially a rustic version of the post and board fence style (pages 150 to 154) and is similarly a good choice for a decorative accent, for delineating areas, or for marking boundaries without creating a solid visual barrier. Typically made from split cedar logs, the fence materials have naturally random shaping and dimensions, with imperfect details and character marks that give the wood an appealing hand-hewn look. Natural weathering of the untreated wood only enhances the fence's rustic beauty.

The construction of a split rail fence couldn't be simpler. The posts have holes or notches (called mortises) cut into one or two facets. The fence rails have trimmed ends (called tenons) that fit into the mortises. No fasteners are needed. Posts come in three types to accommodate any basic configuration: common posts have through mortises, end posts have half-depth mortises on one facet, and corner posts have half-depth mortises on two adjacent facets. The two standard fence styles are two-rail, which stand about 3 feet tall, and three-rail, which stand about

Mason's string	Nails
Shovel	Precut split rail fence posts and rails
Clamshell digger or power auger	Compactable gravel (bank gravel or pea gravel)
Digging bar (with tamping head) or 2 × 4	Plastic tags
Level	Lumber and screws for cross bracing
Reciprocating saw or handsaw	Wheelbarrow
Tape measure	Line level
Stakes	Shovel
Soil	Eye and ear protection
	Work gloves

4 feet tall. Rails are commonly available in 8- and 10-feet lengths.

In keeping with the rustic simplicity of the fence design, split rail fences are typically installed by setting the posts with tamped soil and gravel instead of concrete footings (frost heave is generally not a concern with this fence because the joints allow for plenty of movement). This comes with a few advantages: the postholes are relatively small, you save the expense of concrete, and it's much easier to replace a post if necessary. Plan to bury about a third of the total post length (or 24 inches minimum). This means a 3-foot-tall fence should have 60-inch-long posts. If you can't find long posts at your local home center, try a lumberyard or fencing supplier.

A split rail fence looks great as a garden backdrop or a friendly boundary line. The rough-hewn texture and traditional wood joints are reminiscent of homesteaders' fences built from lumber cut and dressed right on the property.

How to Build a Split Rail Fence

1

Determine the post spacing by dry-assembling a fence section and measuring the distance between the post centers. Be sure the posts are square to the rails before measuring.

2

Set up a string line using mason's string and stakes to establish the fence's path, including any corners and return sections. Mark each post location along the path using a nail and plastic tag.

3

Dig the postholes so they are twice as wide as the posts and at a depth equal to one-third the total post length plus 6". Because split posts vary in size, you might want to lay out the posts beforehand and dig each hole according to the post size.

4

Add 6" of drainage gravel to each posthole. Tamp the gravel thoroughly with a digging bar or a 2 × 4 so the layer is flat and level.

(continued)

Set and measure the first post. Drop the post in its hole, and then hold it plumb while you measure from the ground to the desired height. If necessary, add or remove gravel and re-tamp to adjust the post height.

Brace the post with cross bracing so it is plumb. Add 2" of gravel around the bottom of the post. Tamp the gravel with a digging bar or 2 × 4, being careful not to disturb the post.

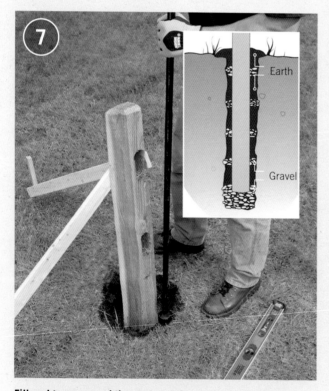

Earth

Gravel

Fill and tamp around the post, one layer at a time. Alternate between 4" of soil and 2" of gravel (inset), tamping each layer all the way around the post before adding the next layer. Check the post for plumb as you work. Overfill the top of the hole with soil and tamp it into a hard mound to help shed water.

Assemble the first section of fence by setting the next post in its hole and checking its height. Fit the rails into the post mortises, and then brace the second post in place.

NOTE: Set all the posts at the same height above grade for a contoured fence. For a level fence, see Variation, right.

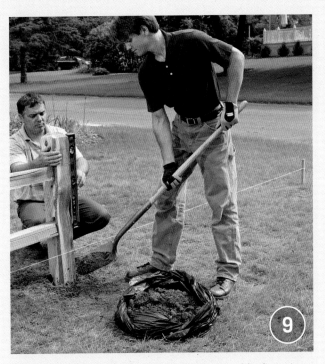

VARIATION: For a fence that remains level across the top, set up a level mason's line strung between two installed fence posts or between temporary supports. Set all of the posts so their tops are just touching the line.

Secure the second post by filling and tamping with alternate layers of gravel and soil, as with the first post. Repeat Steps 5 through 9 to complete the fence.

TIP: Set up a mason's string to help keep the posts in a straight line as you set them.

CUSTOM DETAILS

Loop latch

Pivot hinge

Custom-cut your rails to build shorter fence sections. Cut the rails to length using a reciprocating saw and long wood blade or a handsaw (be sure to factor in the tenon when determining the overall length). To cut the tenon, make a cardboard template that matches the post mortises. Use the template to mark the tenon shape onto the rail end, and then cut the tenon to fit.

Gates for split rail fences are available from fencing suppliers in standard and custom-order sizes. Standard sizes include 4 ft. for a walk-through entrance gate and 8 or 10 ft. for a drive-through gate. For large gates, set the side posts in concrete footings extending below the frost line.

Wood Composite Fence

TOOLS & MATERIALS

Supplies for laying out and setting posts	Composite fence materials and hardware
Drill	Galvanized finish nails or adhesive
Circular saw and carbide-tipped wood blade	Eye and ear protection
Hacksaw	Hammer
Level	Work gloves

Wood composite fencing requires little maintenance and can last a lifetime. For many homeowners, this low-maintenance longevity justifies the high initial cost of the fencing. Manufacturers of composite products claim that they are less expensive than wood in the long run, when you factor in the repair, refinishing, and eventual replacement of wood fences over the years. Quality composite fencing is guaranteed for up to 25 years not to split, crack, splinter, or rot. Perhaps best of all, it never needs to be painted or sealed for protection from the elements.

Composite fences are made from a blend of wood fibers and plastic resins and can contain a high percentage of recycled materials (the country's largest manufacturer of wood composite products uses seven out of every ten grocery bags recycled nationally). Most of the wood used comes from reclaimed sawdust from woodworking industries and discarded shipping pallets. The reuse of waste materials, combined with the fact that the fencing never needs to be finished and may never need to be replaced, makes wood composite one of the most environmentally friendly fence materials available.

Like vinyl fencing, composite systems are assembled from precisely manufactured components and panels. This makes it difficult to modify the length of fence sections, should your post spacing be off. For this reason, you might prefer to set the posts as you go (instead of all at once), using a fence stringer to determine the exact post placement. If your site is sloped, check with the fencing manufacturer for recommendations on stepping or contouring the fence to follow the slope.

Composite fencing is manufactured with a blend of wood fibers and plastic resins. It is denser than vinyl fencing and available in a wide range of colors and textures; some even replicate the look of real wood. The privacy fence above is from the Seclusions line by Trex.

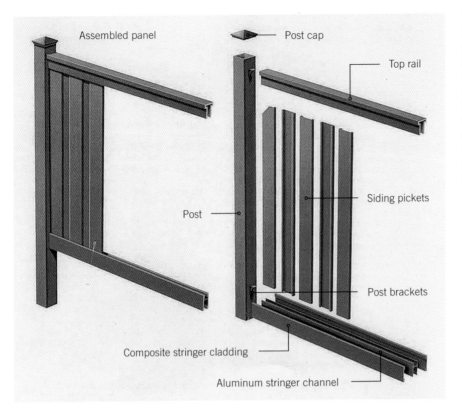

Assembled panel

Post cap

Top rail

Siding pickets

Post

Post brackets

Composite stringer cladding

Aluminum stringer channel

The composite fence system shown in this project is supported by hollow composite posts set in concrete. Bottom stringers include aluminum channels (for strength) clad with composite sleeves. The siding infill is made up of interlocking pieces (or pickets) that fit into the bottom stringer channels and are covered with a top rail. The bottom stringer and top rail are anchored to the posts with brackets.

How to Construct a Wood Composite Fence

Dig the postholes according to your fence layout. Be sure to follow the manufacturer's directions for post spacing. Dig the holes 12" in diameter and 30" deep (or as directed). Add 6" of gravel to each hole and tamp it flat.

Set the posts in concrete using a layout string to ensure precise alignment of the post faces (see page 149). Brace each post with cross bracing so it is perfectly plumb. Fill around the post with concrete, up to 2" below ground level. Tamp the concrete with a 2 × 4 to eliminate air pockets. Let the concrete cure for 24 to 48 hours.

(continued)

Install the post brackets with the provided screws, using the manufacturer's template (inset) to center the brackets on the post faces. Install the bottom bracket onto each post first, measure up from the bracket and mark the position of the top bracket, and then install the top bracket.

Template

Cut a stringer as needed for short sections of fence. Cut the aluminum channel with a hacksaw. Trim the composite cladding pieces to match the channel with a circular saw and carbide-tipped wood blade.

Assemble each bottom stringer by sliding the composite cladding pieces over the sides of the aluminum stringer channel. For short fence sections, see Step 5.

Set the stringer onto the bottom post brackets. Check the stringer with a level. If necessary, remove the stringer and adjust the bracket heights (you may have to adjust top brackets as well to maintain the proper spacing).

Fasten the stringer ends to the post brackets using the provided screws.

Trim the upper outside corner of the first picket so it will clear the top post bracket using a circular saw and carbide-tipped wood blade.

Install the first picket by slipping its bottom end into the stringer channel. Align the picket to the top post bracket, and fasten the picket to the post with three evenly spaced screws.

Fit the last picket into place after trimming its top corner to clear the post bracket, as you did with the first panel. Fasten the picket to the post with three screws, as in Step 9.

Assemble the fence panel by fitting the pickets together along their interlocking side edges and sliding their bottom ends into the stringer channel.

Set the top rail over the ends of the pickets until the rail meets the top post brackets.

Secure the top rail to each top post bracket, using the provided screws, driving the screws through the top of the rail and into the bracket.

Add the post caps, securing them to the posts with galvanized finish nails or an approved adhesive.

TIP: Some fence manufacturers offer more than one cap style (inset).

Vinyl Panel Fence

The best features of vinyl fencing are its resilience and durability. Vinyl fencing is made with a form of tough, weather-resistant, UV-protected PVC (polyvinyl chloride), a plastic compound that's found in numerous household products, from plumbing pipe to shower curtains. A vinyl fence never needs to be painted and should be guaranteed for decades not to rot, warp, or discolor. So if you like the styling of traditional wood fences, but minimal maintenance is a primary consideration, vinyl might just be your best option. Another good option is wood composite fencing (see pages 160 to 163), which comes in fewer styles than vinyl but is environmentally friendly and can replicate the look of wood fencing.

Installing most vinyl fencing is similar to building a wood panel fence. With both materials, it's safest to set the posts as you go, using the infill panels to help you position the posts. Accurate post placement is critical with vinyl, because many types of panels cannot be trimmed if the posts are too close together. Squeezing the panel in can lead to buckling when the vinyl expands on hot days, while setting the posts too far apart results in unsightly gaps.

Given the limited workability of most vinyl panels, this fencing tends to work best on level or gently sloping ground. Keep in mind that installation of vinyl fences varies widely by manufacturer and fence style.

TOOLS & MATERIALS

Mason's string

Shovel

Clamshell digger or power auger

Circular saw

Drill

Tape measure

Hand maul

Line level

Post level

Clamps or duct tape

Concrete tools

Stakes

2 × 4 lumber

Vinyl fence materials
(with hardware, fasteners, and decorative accessories)

Pea gravel

Concrete

Pressure-treated 4 × 4
(for gate, if applicable)

PVC cement or screws (optional)

Work gloves

Post caps

Eye and ear protection

Vinyl fencing is now available in a wide range of traditional designs, including picket, post and board, open rail, and solid panel. Color options are generally limited to various shades of white, tan, and gray.

How to Install a Vinyl Panel Fence

Lay out the first run of fence with stakes and mason's string. Position the string so it represents the outside or inside faces of the posts (you'll use layout strings to align the posts throughout the installation). Mark the center of the first post hole by measuring in from the string half the post width.

Attach the fence panel brackets to the first post using the provided screws. Dry-fit a fence panel into the brackets, then measure from the top of the post to the bottom edge of the panel. Add 2" (or as directed) to represent the distance between the fence and the ground; the total dimension is the posts' height above the ground.

Dig the first posthole, following the manufacturer's requirements for diameter and depth (improper hole dimensions can void the warranty). Add 4" to 6" (or as directed) of pea gravel to the bottom of the hole and tamp it down so it is flat and level using a 2 × 4 or 4 × 4.

Set up a post-top string to guide the post installation. Using the post height dimension, tie a mason's string between temporary 2 × 4 supports so the string is centered over the post locations. Use a line level to make sure the string is level. Measure from the string to the ground in several places to make sure the height is suitable along the entire fence run.

(continued)

Set the first post. Drop the post in its hole and align it with the fence line string and height string. Install cross bracing to hold the post perfectly plumb.

TIP: Secure bracing boards to the post with spring-type clamps or duct tape. Fill the posthole with concrete and let it set completely.

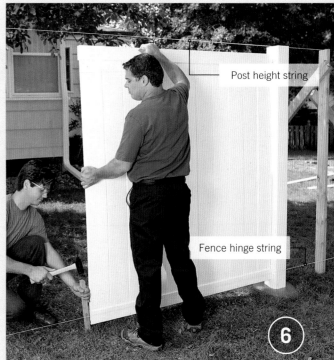

Post height string

Fence hinge string

Determine the second post's location by fitting a fence panel into the brackets on the first post. Mark the ground at the free edge of the panel. Measure out from the mark half the post width to find the center of the post hole (accounting for any additional room needed for the panel brackets).

Complete the fence section. Dig the hole for the second post, add gravel, and tamp as before. Attach the panel brackets to the second post, set the post in place, and check its height against the string line. Assemble the fence section with the provided screws (inset). Confirm that the fence panel is level. Brace the second post in place (as shown) and anchor it with concrete. Repeat the same layout and construction steps to build the remaining fence sections.

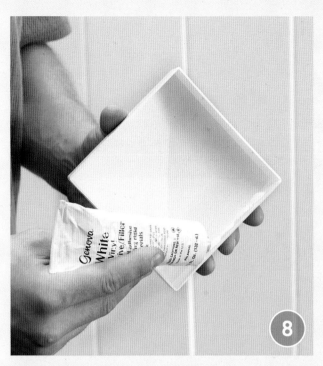

Cut panels for short runs on solid-panel fencing (if straight along the top) per manufacturer's recommendations.

Add the post caps. Depending on the product, caps may be installed with PVC cement or screws, or they may be fitted without fasteners. Add any additional decorative accessories, such as screw caps, to complete the installation.

Installing a Vinyl Fence Gate

Hang the gate using the provided hardware. Fasten the hinges to the gate panel with screws. Position the gate in line with the infill fence panels and screw the hinges to the hinge post. Install the latch hardware onto the gate and latch post. Close the gate, position the gate stops against the gate rails, and fasten the stops to the latch post with screws.

POST INFILLS

Reinforce the hinge post with a pressure-treated 4 × 4 inserted inside the post. Set the post in concrete following the same steps used for fence sections. Check carefully to make sure the post is plumb, as this will ensure the gate swings properly. Install the latch post according to the manufacturer's specified dimension for the gate opening.

Ornamental Metal Fence

Ornamental metal fencing is so called to distinguish it from the other common metal fence material, chain link, which makes a useful fence, but is far from ornamental. Ornamental metal fences arguably offer the best combination of strength, durability, and visibility of any standard fence type. In general, most ornamental metal fences are modern iterations of traditional iron, or "wrought iron," fencing and offer a similarly elegant, formal look (if perhaps not the same heft and handcrafted character).

Today, most ornamental metal fencing is made with galvanized steel or aluminum. Both are finished with durable powder coatings for weather resistance, and most fence systems are based on modular components designed for easy DIY installation. Comparing the two materials, appearances are virtually identical, while aluminum is lighter in weight. It also tends to carry a longer warranty than steel products, probably because aluminum is a naturally rust-proof material. The other type of ornamental fence is iron, which is available in a variety of forms, including bolt-together modular systems.

Thanks to its exceptional security and visibility, ornamental metal fencing is a very popular choice for upscale yards. That's why most manufacturers offer gates (with welded construction for strength) and code-compliant locking hardware as standard options. Some fence lines include special infill panels and gates with closer picket spacing than standard panels. If you're installing your fence as a pool surround, check the local codes for requirements.

TOOLS & MATERIALS

Tools and materials for setting posts	Modular fence materials
Mason's string	Concrete
Tape measure	Lumber and screws for cross bracing
Shovel	Wheelbarrow
Clamshell digger or power auger	Masking tape
Clamps or duct tape	Marking paint
Drill	Level
Concrete tools	Hacksaw
Post level	Drainage gravel
Stakes	Eye and ear protection
2 × 4 or 4 × 4 lumber	Work gloves
	1 × 3 or 1 × 4 lumber
	Permanent marker

Ornamental steel, aluminum, and iron fences come in prefabricated panels up to 6 ft. in height and 8 ft. in length, with matching posts and optional decorative details. The most common color option is black (the better to mimic the look of wrought iron), but some products come in white, bronze, and other colors.

How to Install an Ornamental Metal Fence

Mark the first post location with ground-marking spray paint. Assemble the panel onto the first post and align it in the corner with the mason's strings.

Lay out the fence line with stakes and mason's string. Start at the corners, driving stakes a few feet beyond the actual corner so that the strings intersect at 90° (as applicable). Mark the approximate post locations onto the strings using tape or a marker.

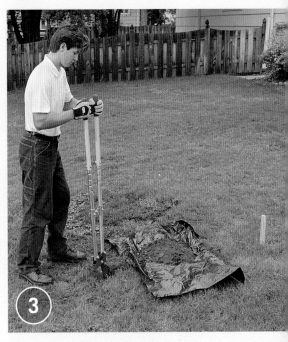

Dig the first posthole, following the manufacturer's specifications for depth and diameter. Shovel drainage gravel into the hole, and tamp it with a 2 × 4 or 4 × 4. Set the post in the hole and measure its height above the ground. If necessary, add or remove gravel until the post top is at the recommended height.

First post

Post level

Plumb and anchor the first post. Position the post perfectly plumb using a post level. Brace the post with cross bracing. Use clamps to secure the bracing to the post. Fill the hole with concrete and let it set.

Drill pilot holes for the brackets into the second post and first panel. Align the fence assembly with the first post and mark for the second post hole. Prepare the posthole as you did in Step 3.

(continued)

Fill the second posthole with concrete and let it set. Here, we have a temporary brace to hold the post plumb and at the desired height. The first panel, complete with posts on either sides, is now set. Remaining posts along this fence line can be set by positioning posts with spacers to save time (see tip on this page).

Align the second panel on the other side of the corner post. Follow instructions in Steps 2 through 5 to set the post and install the panel. Repeat the same process to install the remaining fence sections. You can save time by positioning the posts with spacers (see tip on this page).

SPACING POSTS

Spacers help you locate the posts without having to measure or install each panel for every post. The panels are then added after the post concrete has set. Create each spacer with two 1 × 3 or 1 × 4 boards. Cut board(s) to fit flush from outside edge to outside edge of the first and second post (once they are set in concrete). Clamp the board in between an anchored post and the next post to be installed. It is best to position spacer boards near the top and bottom of the posts. With the boards in place, the linear spacing should be accurate, but always check the new post with a level to make sure it is plumb before setting it in concrete. Use a level mason's string to keep the post brackets at the same elevation.

VARIATION: For brick pillar corners, columns, or the side of a house, install manufacturer-provided wall brackets. If wall brackets do not come with the standard installation package of your metal fence, contact the manufacturer.

How to Cut Metal

Measure and mark panels for cuts. Hold the panel up to the final post in the run and mark the cutting line. Often, designs will not accommodate full panels around the entire fence perimeter.

Cut panels to the appropriate length using a hacksaw, as needed.

OLD (AND OLD-FASHIONED) IRON FENCING

Traditional iron fencing—commonly called "wrought iron"—has been adorning and securing homes and other buildings for many centuries and is still the gold standard of ornamental metal fencing. The oldest forms of wrought iron fences were made with individually hand-forged pieces, while cast-iron fences were assembled from interchangeable pieces of molded iron. Wrought iron, the material, is a pure form of iron that contains very little carbon. Most modern iron fences are made of a form of steel, not wrought iron.

While new iron fencing can still be made by the hand of a blacksmith, it's also commonly available in preassembled panels and modular posts, much like the steel and aluminum fencing sold at home centers. Some iron fencing must be welded together on-site (by professional installers), while some is assembled with bolts, making it suitable for DIY installation. Many styles of prefab iron fencing can be surprisingly affordable.

If you have your heart set on the timeless look and feel of iron, search online for local fabricators and dealers of real iron fencing. You can also hunt through local architectural salvage shops, where you can find antique iron fence panels, posts, finials, and other adornments. Their condition may not be perfect, but the patina of weathering and marks of use only add to the character of old iron fencing.

Whether it was made yesterday or in the 1800s, iron fencing offers enduring beauty and unmatched durability, making it worth the splurge on a small fence or a front entry gate.

Bamboo Fence

TOOLS & MATERIALS

Circular saw or reciprocating saw	Deck screws (3", 2½", 2")
Drill/driver	Bamboo fence panels with ¾"-dia. canes
Countersink bit	Level
Wire cutters	Tape measure
Pliers	Eye and ear protection
Posthole digger	Galvanized steel wire
Lumber (4 × 4, 2 × 4, 1 × 4, 2 × 6)	Work gloves

Bamboo is one of nature's best building materials. It's lightweight, naturally rot resistant, and so strong that it's used for scaffolding in many parts of the world. It's also a highly sustainable resource, since many species can be harvested every 3 to 5 years without destroying the plants. Yet, perhaps the best feature of bamboo is its appearance—whether it's lined up in orderly rows or hand-tied into decorative patterns, bamboo fencing has an exotic, organic quality that adds a breath of life to any setting.

Bamboo is a grass, but it shares many properties with wood. It can be cut, drilled, and sanded with the same tools, and it takes many of the same finishes, including stains and exterior sealers. And, just like wood, bamboo is prone to splitting, though it retains much of its strength even when subject to large splits and cracks. In general,

larger-diameter poles (which can be upwards of 5 inches) are more likely to split than smaller (such as ¾-inch-diameter) canes.

Bamboo fencing is commonly available in 8-foot-long panels made from similarly sized canes held together with internal or external wires. The panels, which are rolled up for easy transport, can be used as infill within a new wood framework or they can attach directly to an existing wood or metal fence. Both of these popular applications are shown here. Another option is to build an all-bamboo fence using large bamboo poles for the posts and stringers and roll-up panels for the infill.

Quality bamboo for fencing isn't hard to find, but you can't pick it up at your local lumberyard. The best place to start shopping is the internet (see Resources, page 234). Look for well-established suppliers who are committed to sustainable practices. Most suppliers can ship product directly to your home.

How to Build a Wood-Frame Bamboo Fence

Install and trim the 4 × 4 posts according to the size of your bamboo panels, setting the posts in concrete. For the 6 × 8-ft. panels in this project, the posts are spaced 100" on-center and are trimmed at 75" tall (refer to the manufacturer's recommendations).

Install the top 2 × 4 stringers. Cut each stringer to fit snugly between the posts. Position the stringer on edge so it is flush with the tops of the posts and with the back or front faces of the posts. Fasten the stringer with 3" deck screws driven through angled pilot holes. Use one screw on each edge and one on the inside face of the stringer, at both ends.

Mark the location of each bottom stringer. The span between the top of the top stringer and bottom of the bottom stringer should equal the bamboo panel height plus about 1". Cut and install the bottom stringers in the same fashion as the top stringers. Here, the bottom stringer will be installed 2" above the ground for rot prevention. Unroll the bamboo panels.

Flatten the bamboo panels over the inside faces of the stringers. Make sure the panels fit the frames on all sides. Using a countersink-piloting bit (inset), drill a slightly countersunk pilot hole through a bamboo cane and into the stringer at a top corner of the panel. Fasten the corner with a 2" deck screw, being careful not to overtighten and split the bamboo. *(continued)*

Screws

2 × 4

⑤

Fasten the rest of the panel with screws spaced 12" apart. Stagger the screws top and bottom and drive them in an alternating pattern, working from one side to the other. Repeat Steps 4 and 5 to install the remaining bamboo panels.

To shorten the length of a bamboo panel, cut the wiring holding the canes together at least two canes beyond the desired length using wire cutters. Remove the extra canes and then wrap the loose ends of wire around the last cane in the panel.

Add the top cap. Center the 2 × 6 top cap boards over the posts so they overhang about 1" on either side. Fasten the caps to the posts and stringers with 3" deck screws. Use miter joints for corners, and use scarf joints (cut with opposing 30° or 45° bevels) to join cap boards over long runs.

⑥

Cover the top and bottom ends of the panels with 1 × 4 battens. These finish off the panels and give the fence a similar look on both sides. Cut the battens so the ends are flush against the inside faces of the posts and fasten them to the panels and stringers with 2½" deck screws driven through pilot holes.

⑦

How to Cover an Old Fence with Bamboo

Unroll and position a bamboo panel over one or both sides of the existing fence. Check the panel with a level and adjust as needed. For rot prevention, hold the panel 1" to 2" above the ground.

TIP: A 2 × 4 laid flat on the ground makes it easy to prop up and level the panel.

Fasten the panel with deck screws driven through the bamboo canes (and fence siding boards, if applicable) and into the fence stringers. Drill countersunk pilot holes for the screws, being careful not to overtighten and crack the bamboo. Space the screws 12" apart, and stagger them top and bottom (see facing page).

Install the remaining bamboo panels, butting the edges together between panels for a seamless appearance. If the fence posts project above the stringer boards, you can cut the bamboo panels flush with the posts.

VARIATION: To dress up a chain-link fence with bamboo fencing, simply unroll the panels over the fence and secure them every 12" or so with short lengths of galvanized steel wire. Tie the wire around the canes or the panel wiring and over the chain-link mesh.

Water Features

Is it possible to deny the allure of water? Not really. If there is any body of water nearby—a lake, a pond, a river, a stream—then all creatures great and small are drawn to it. That's just a given. And if that body of water is in your backyard? Heaven!

This chapter is going to help you create some landscaping heaven in the form of a water feature. Water features instantly activate your senses. Their beauty holds your eye and sets the mood for calm and contemplation—not to mention great conversation. Their musical sounds of trickling and gurgling mask ambient, urban noise and produce "laughing waters" that lift your mood. And on hot days, dipping your toes in their cool waters brings on the ahhs.

By building one of the three projects included in this chapter, you will create your own oasis, a flowing or reflective focal point that will sparkle as the jewel of your backyard. It will pull in a new class of plants and animals (birds, fish) for your enjoyment, and it will class up your property with the look of landscaping luxury.

In This Chapter:
- Designing Water Features
- Hard-shell Pond & Fountain
- Small Gazing Pond
- Waterfall & Pond

Designing Water Features

Like many activities, success in water gardening is rooted in good preparation. Good planning is essential to reaping the full rewards of a water feature and adequately nurturing aquatic plants. While it may be motivating to pick up a shovel and start digging out a streambed, knowing how that step fits into the overall project makes the process easier and more successful.

At first glance, it may be obvious where a water garden fits into your landscape. It's a good idea, however, to confirm a proper location using the following criteria:

Grade: Place ponds or pools on level ground near the highest point in the yard, a place high above the water table and safe from any runoff. Streams or watercourses are best on gentle slopes.

Climate: Water gardens need 5 to 6 hours of sun daily.

Soil: Sample soil at your proposed site to determine its type. Clay soil provides a stable base for pond and pool liners. Plan to stabilize sandy soil before installing a liner.

Utilities: Have utility lines marked by your utility providers. Move or adjust the dimensions or even the site of the water garden so it doesn't interfere with the utility lines.

Concept to Design

Create a garden plan on graph paper or using a computer software program developed for landscape design. Begin with a base plan to indicate everything that exists on your site now. Start with a copy of your property's survey for an accurate rendering—they're usually available from the local building department—or measure your property and carefully transfer the distances to scaled graph paper. Mark the placement of your home, other permanent structures, and features you plan to retain on the site: existing trees, planting beds, paths, and decks or patios. Mark the location of all underground utility lines. Accurately record the dimensions and locations of these components. Add to this the information you've discovered about your garden: the sun and shade pattern, the wind direction, and any changes of elevation on your site. Make some photocopies of the site drawing and sketch out possible water features on them.

Siting and sizing a water feature is usually pretty easy: once you've considered all of the factors and requirements for building one, including local codes, the process of elimination won't leave many options.

How to Draw a Water Feature Plan

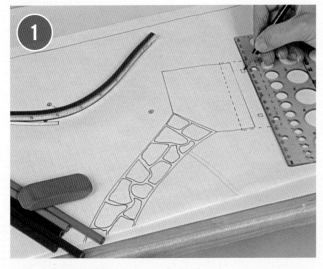

On scaled graph paper, draw the site and its measurements in the general area of the feature. Include existing structures, trees, and all utility lines, plus changes of elevation. This is your base plan.

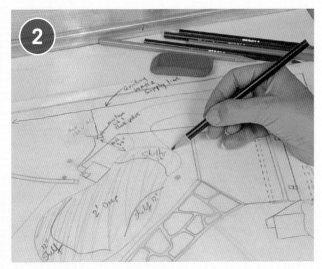

On a tissue paper overlay or photocopy, experiment with different options for your feature's location, style, and structure until you're satisfied.

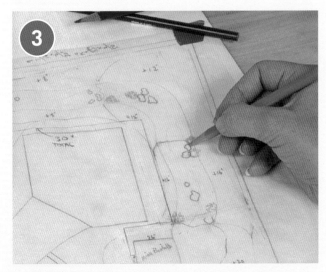

Transfer your final measurements to a clean overlay. Draw electrical supplies and water sources, the path of your recirculating pipe, and the position of the skimmer intake and water discharge.

Use colored pencils to mark edge materials and landscape plant choices around the pond. Remember that the pond requires full sun and access. Next, choose aquatic plants and indicate their planting points.

Transfer your plant selections to a list for easy reference and for use when you visit your aquatic nursery. Note your plant requirements, including bloom color, season of bloom, variety, selection, and care needs.

Hard-Shell Pond & Fountain

A small pond and fountain add more than the illusion of luxury to landscapes; they also add the sound and sparkle of moving water and invite birds to join the party. Installing a pond and fountain can be heavy work, but it's not at all complicated. If you can use a shovel and read a level, you can install a beautiful fountain like the classic Roman fountain shown here.

Most freestanding fountains are designed to be set into an independently installed water feature. The fountains typically are preplumbed with an integral pump, but larger ones may have an external pumping apparatus. The kind of kit you'll find at your local building or garden center normally comes in at least two parts: the pedestal and the vessel.

The project shown here falls into the luxury-you-can-afford category and is fully achievable for a DIYer. If the project you have in mind is of massive scale (with a pond larger than around 8 × 10 ft.) you'll likely need to work with a pondscaping professional to acquire and install the materials needed for such an endeavor.

You can install a fountain in an existing water feature, or you can build a new one with a hard liner, as shown here, or with a soft liner (see pages 187 to 189). Have your utility providers mark the locations of all utility lines before beginning this or any project that involves digging.

TOOLS & MATERIALS

Level
Shovel or spade
Hand tamp
Rope
Preformed pond liner
Sand
Compactable gravel
Interlocking paving stones
Rubber floor mat
Free-standing fountain
Fountain pedestal
Tarp
River stones

The work necessary to install a garden pond and fountain will pay dividends for many years to come. The process is not complicated, but does involve some fairly heavy labor, such as digging and hauling stones.

Installing Ponds & Fountains

A hard shell-type liner combines well with a fountain because its flat, hard bottom makes a stable surface for resting the fountain base. You may need to prop up the fountain to get it to the optimal level. Note: Most municipalities require that permanent water features be surrounded by a structure, fence, or wall on all sides to keep small children from wandering in. Good designers view this as a creative challenge, rather than an impediment.

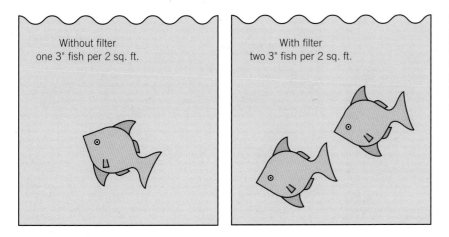

Without filter
one 3" fish per 2 sq. ft.

With filter
two 3" fish per 2 sq. ft.

If you plan to stock your pond with plant life or livestock, it's important to keep a healthy balance. For stocking with fish, the pond must be at least 24" deep, and you should have at least one submerged water plant to create oxygen.

Choose a flat area of your yard. Set the hard-shell pond liner right-side up in the installation area and adjust it until you are pleased with the location (it should be well away from buried utility lines). Hold a level against the edge of the top of the liner and use it as a guide to transfer the liner shape onto the ground below with a rope.

Cut away the sod within the outline. Measure the liner at the center and excavate the base area to this depth. Dig the hole 2" to 3" deeper than the liner, and dig past the outline a couple of inches all the way around. If the sides of your liner are sloped, slope the edges of the hole to match.

Remove any rocks or debris on the bottom of the hole and add sand to cover the bottom of the hole about 2" deep. Test fit the liner and adjust the sand until the underside of the liner rim is slightly above ground and the liner is level from side to side.

Cut away the sod beyond the liner excavation area and dig out an area wide enough to accommodate your paving stones (called coping stones), about 1" deeper than the average stone thickness. Flagstone is the most common natural stone choice for coping because it is flat; concrete pavers also may be used easily. Make sure the surface of the excavation is as level as possible.

5

Fill the liner with 4" to 6" of water. Fill the space between the liner and the sides of the hole with damp sand, using a 2 × 4 to tamp it down as you go. Add more water and then more sand; continue until the pond and the gap are filled.

6

Bail about half of the water out of the pond. Place an exterior-rated rubber floor mat (or mats) at least ½" thick on the liner in the spot where you'd like the fountain to rest.

7

Feed the fountain's power cord up through the access holes in the pedestal. Set the fountain in place on top of the pedestal and run the cord to the edge.

8

Check to make sure the pedestal is level. If necessary, shim the pedestal with small flat stones to make the fountain level.

(continued)

Set interlocking pavers in place around the lip of the liner. Adjust compactable gravel as necessary to make the pavers level. Add 1" to 3" of water to stabilize the liner.

Cover the pond and pedestal with a clean tarp and add an inch of compactable gravel to the excavated area for the paving stones. Tamp down the gravel and check the area with a level. Cut a small channel for the power cord and route it beyond the excavated area toward a power source.

Cover the bottom of the liner with washed river rock. Place the fountain onto the pedestal and submerge the cord, running it out of the pond in an inconspicuous spot, such as between two pavers.

Ponds look more natural if you line the bottoms with rock. Small-diameter (2" to 3") river rock is a good choice. Before putting it into the pond, rinse the rock well. One trick is to put the nozzle of a hose in the bottom of a clean 5-gal. bucket and then fill the bucket with dirty rock. Turn on the hose and let the water run for 15 minutes or so. This will cause impurities to float up and out of the bucket.

Allow the water to settle for 30 minutes or so, and then turn on the fountain pump and test. Let the pump run for an hour or so, and then turn it off and remove the fountain head. Use a hose and spray nozzle to clear out any blockages. Perform this maintenance regularly and whenever you notice that the spray from the fountain seems to be restricted.

Completely fill both the pond and the fountain's base with water. If you will not be stocking the pond with fish or plants, add 2 oz. of chlorine bleach for every 10 gal. of water.

POWER CORD MANAGEMENT

There are many ways to provide electrical power to operate the fountain pump. The best way is to add a new outdoor circuit, but this requires an electrician if you are not experienced with home wiring. The easier route is to feed your fountain pump with an exterior-rated extension cord that's plugged into an existing outdoor receptacle. Because having an extension cord laying in your lawn is both a tripping hazard and an electrical hazard (lawn mowers and wiring do not get along), you can bury the cord in a shallow trench. To protect it from digging instruments, either backfill with rocks so you know the exact location of the cord, or bury it encased in heavy conduit.

Avoid using this tactic if the pond is located more than 50 feet from the power source.

Dig a trench about 6" deep and 6" wide from the pond to your outdoor power source.

Feed the cord through conduit and lay the conduit in the trench all the way from the pond to the power source. Backfill the trench with dirt.

Small Gazing Pond

TOOLS & MATERIALS

Level

Shovel or spade

Hand tamp

Tape measure

Garden hose or rope

Spray paint

Pond underlayment

Flexible pond liner

Sand

Compactable gravel

Flagstone pavers

River rocks

Plants (optional)

Fish (optional)

A tranquil reflecting pond serves as a focal point in an outdoor room and a fertile setting for water-loving plants. A pond's shape can take on any configuration if you use a soft, pliable pond liner. Once complete, your pond will become an anchor for additional landscape elements, such as a bridge, or stonescaping by placing appealing natural rock as a border.

EPDM (ethylene propylene diene monomer) liners are made from a synthetic rubber that is highly flexible, extremely durable, and fish-friendly. EPDM liners remain flexible at temperatures ranging from -40 to 175 degrees Fahrenheit. These are cost-effective and easy to find at building or garden centers or landscape supply stores. Look for a liner that is 45 mil thick. Some landscape supply centers carry pond liner by the lineal foot.

Free-form ponds blend into the landscape, especially with the addition of coping stones set into the edges. Building one involves heavy labor but no special skills.

How to Create a Freeform Garden Pond

SIZING YOUR LINER

Flexible liners adapt to nearly any shape or size pond you want. They can fit a typical kidney-shaped excavation with planting shelves, like the one shown here, or a very unique shape of your own design. EPDM rubber liner material is sold in precut sizes at your local home and garden center.

Select a location well away from buried utility lines. Use a garden hose or a rope to outline the pond. Avoid very sharp turns, and try for a natural looking configuration. When you're satisfied with the pond's shape, lift the hose or rope and use spray paint to mark the perimeter.

Find the lowest point on the perimeter and flag it for reference as the elevation benchmark. This represents the top of the pond's water-holding capacity, so all depth measurements should be taken from this point. Start digging at the deepest point (usually the middle of the pond) and work out toward the edges. For border plantings, establish one 6"- to 8"-wide ledge about 12" down from the benchmark.

Set a level on the plant shelf to confirm that it is the same elevation throughout. Unless your building site is perfectly level or you have done a lot of earth moving, the edges of the pond are not likely to be at the same elevation, so there may be some pond liner visible between the benchmark and the high point. This can usually be concealed with plants, rocks, or by overhanging your coping more in high areas.

(continued)

Dig a 4"-deep by 12"-wide frame around the top of the hole to make room for the coping stones (adjust the width if you are using larger stones). Remove any rocks, debris, roots, or anything sharp in the hole, and add a 2" layer of sand to cover the bottom of the frame.

Cover the bottom and sides of the excavation with pond underlayment. Pond underlayment is a shock-absorbing, woven fabric that you should be able to buy from the same source that provides your liner. If necessary, cut triangles of underlayment and fit them together, overlapping pieces as necessary to cover the contours. This is not a waterproof layer.

Lay out the liner material and let it warm in the sun for an hour or two. Arrange the liner to cover the excavation, folding and overlapping as necessary. Place rocks around the edges to keep it from sliding into the hole.

Begin filling the pond with water. Watch the liner as the water level gets higher, and adjust and tuck it to minimize sharp folds and empty pockets.

Add some larger stones to the pond as the water rises, including a flat stone for your pond pump/filter. If the pump/filter has a fountain feature, locate it near the center. If not, locate it near the edge in an easy-to-reach spot.

Fill the pond all the way to the top until it overflows at the benchmark. Remove the stones holding the liner in place and begin laying flat stones, such as flagstones, around the perimeter of the pond. Cut and trim flagstones as necessary to minimize gaps.

Finish laying the coping stones and fill in gaps with cutoff and shards. If you are in a temperate climate, consider mortaring the coping stones, but be very careful to keep wet mortar out of the water: it kills plants and damages pump/filters. Set flagstone pavers on the ledge at the perimeter of the pond. Add more water and adjust the liner again. Fill the pond to just below the flagstones and trim the liner.

Consult a garden center, an extension agent from a local university, or the Internet to help you choose plants for your pond. Include a mixture of deep-water plants, marginals, oxygenators, and floating plants. Place the plants in the pond. If necessary to bring them to the right height, set the plants on bricks or flat stones. Spread decorative gravel, sand, or mulch to cover the liner at the perimeter of the pond. Install plants along the pond's margins, if desired.

Waterfall & Pond

Water gardening is a popular form of landscaping, offering the prospect of peace and tranquility, along with some property enhancement potential. If you've thought about jumping in but feared you might end up in a sea of maintenance problems, check out this pond project and dive on in—the water's fine! It's an elaborate and beautiful pond, but perhaps best of all it is virtually self-sustaining and maintenance free.

The reason this water feature does not require the level of maintenance that a typical pump-and-filter based system needs is that this one mimics nature. And a water feature that successfully mimics nature's ecosystem can free you from chores such as monitoring water quality, balancing chemicals, repairing leaks, and nursing sick plants and fish.

How It Works

The process is simple, but it does involve heavy labor. In a nutshell, you dig holes for the pond and bog, carve a streambed, line it all with fabric and a waterproof liner, add culverts, a pump, rocks, and water, and finish with plants and fish. A healthy water feature requires a combination of components. The bog/pond design featured here achieves a balance because it includes a cascading stream and a bog garden as well as vegetation and fish. As water flows through the system, it is aerated and filtered—just as a natural stream would be.

SEVEN ESSENTIALS TO A SELF-SUSTAINING POND

To create a self-sustaining ecosystem, incorporate these elements into your water feature:

1. Circulation—Stagnant water is dirty and a breeding ground for mosquitoes. In a healthy pond, water is circulated through the system, is aerated as it cascades downstream, and is filtered as it pushes through rock beds. Moving water also delivers nutrients to plants.

2. Mechanical filter—The mechanical filter of this bog system is the pump, which moves water and carries debris to the bog filtration tube.

3. Biological filter—Rock and plant material (not chemicals) clean the water as it passes through the system.

4. Bacteria—Beneficial bacteria are nature's recycling agents. They consume fish waste and debris, converting deadly ammonia to useful nitrogen that feeds plants. To jump-start the bacteria level in a new water feature (and at spring start-up), some pond experts treat the water with microbial bacteria additives, but bacteria will build on its own in most cases, and the system will balance itself in time.

5. Rocks—Besides making a water feature attractive, rocks add considerable surface area where bacteria can grow, and they provide pockets for plants to root and fish to hide. They also hold the liner in position and protect it from UV exposure.

6. Plants—To help control algae, plants block sunlight and compete for the same nutrients that algae thrive upon. Plants also provide food and habitat for fish.

7. Fish—These animals eat mosquito larvae, debris, and insects. Their waste supports plant life and enhances growth of beneficial bacteria. Best of all, they add color and provide entertainment.

It's easy to plan the size, shape, and location of a water feature to fit your yard's available space and landscaping. This 6 × 8-foot pond is relatively small because it was made to fit within an existing fenced area. But with more space and materials (and energy), you can build a water feature as large as you want. In fact, larger is better because a higher volume of water keeps the system more easily balanced.

This bog/stream/pond works well on either a flat area or a hill. The one shown here was built on a slope that has a total drop of less than 2 feet.

Whatever the grade, create a series of steps down rather than one or two large falls to minimize water loss.

To achieve a natural look, we chose an irregular shape for the outline of our water feature. If you want a formal water garden, you could choose a more symmetrical or a geometric shape and use materials such as brick or uniform stones.

Before you decide on a site, check local codes regarding setback distances, fence requirements, and electrical permits, and have all utilities' locations marked so you don't hit any pipes or cables during excavation.

Locate your pond near a water supply and an exterior-rated electrical outlet (equipped with a GFCI). Consult an electrician if you need to add an outlet.

Because most water-garden plants like plenty of sunlight, avoid heavily shaded areas. Overhanging branches also drop leaves, twigs, blossoms, and seeds into the water.

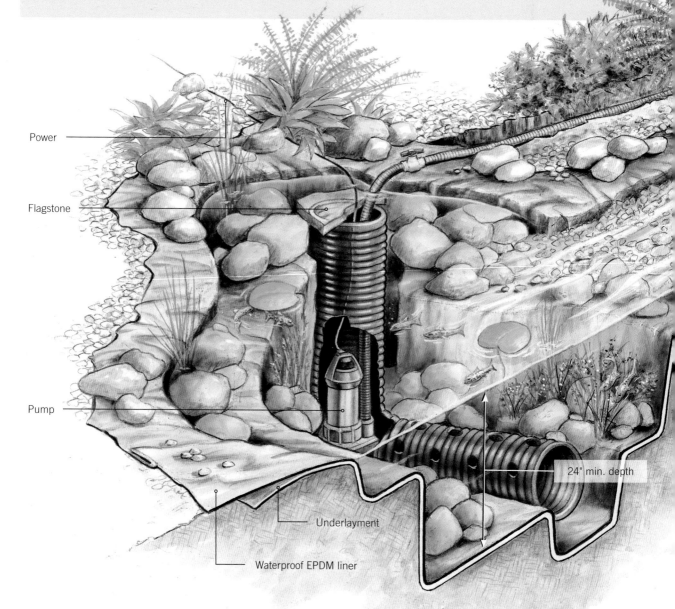

Power

Flagstone

Pump

Underlayment

24" min. depth

Waterproof EPDM liner

The pump sends water from the pond through the flexible PVC tubing to the floor of the bog. Debris and sediment collect in the elbow of the bog culvert, and the water is cleaned by biological filtration as it flows upward through a perforated culvert, rocks, gravel, and plants. From there the filtered water is aerated as it cascades down to the pond.

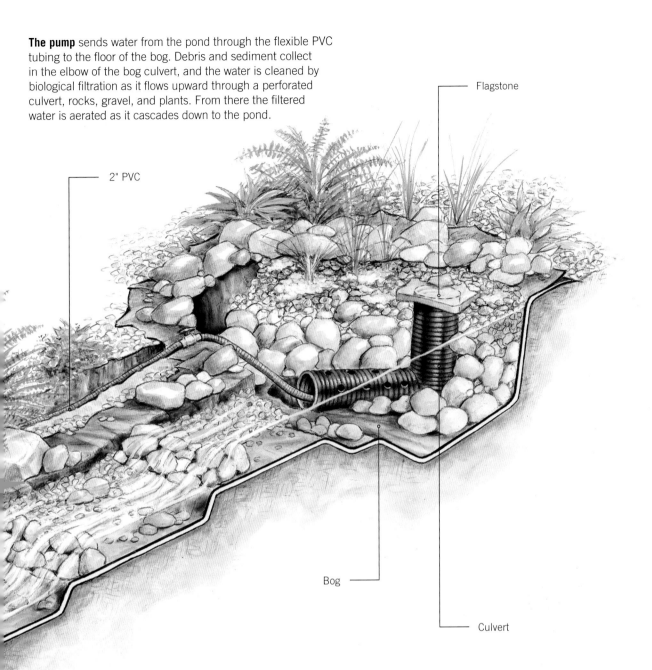

2" PVC

Flagstone

Bog

Culvert

POND SYSTEM COMPONENTS

- Filtration tubes—12-inch-diameter polyethylene corrugated culvert (A) and two 90-degree elbows (B), available at farm supply stores, to house the pump in the pond and hold debris in the bog.

- Flexible 2-inch PVC (C)—This tubing carries the water from the pump to the floor of the bog. Two 2-inch ball shutoff valves (D), a 2-inch coupler (E), and hose clamps.

- Submersible pump (F)—For proper filtration and aeration, the water must turn over at least once every two hours. Calculate the cubic feet of your water feature and multiply that number by 7.5, which is the number of gallons each cubic foot holds.

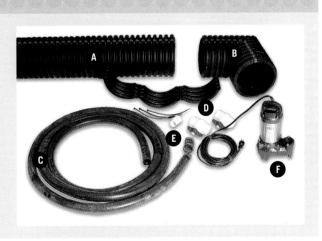

How to Make a Waterfall & Pond

Lay out the outline of your planned garden. To visualize the pond's design, use a garden hose to outline a shape. Trace the outline with spray paint and then remove the hose. Use a rod and a transit level to find the lowest edge of the pond. The pond's perimeter should vary in height for a natural look, but you need to create one low edge so that overflow due to heavy rains and snowmelt will be directed away from nearby structures. Use the low spot as a benchmark for establishing pond depth.

Berm

Outline for next level

Excavate the pond, bog, and streambed. You'll use some of the soil to landscape around the water feature, but you'll probably need a spot (nearby if possible) to deposit the leftovers. To prevent settling, tamp any soil that is added to or disturbed within your water garden area. Dig within the outlined shape of the pond, grading the entire inside area to be level with a point that is 8" below the benchmark. (Most edges of the pond will be more than 8" high.) About 10" to 16" from the edge, outline and dig a second level at least 8" deeper. Create the resulting tier to vary in width and have a slight grade toward the center of the pond so debris will flow toward the pump. The shelf provides a home for plants and a spot for people to safely step in or out of the pond if necessary.

Shape and finish each tier before marking and digging the next step down. With a surveyor's level, determine that the shelf area is at the same elevation all around. Also check that each tier slopes slightly toward the center of the pond. You can carve a third level in the center if your pond is larger; just be sure you reach a total depth of at least 24"—the minimum depth for fish to survive winter in a northern climate. Finally, dig a 10"-deep × 16"-wide trench across the pond floor to hold the culvert tube. Grade the trench slightly downward toward the pump end.

Pond

Trench for 2" PVC

④

Stream

Holding pond

Bog

Trench for culvert

Next, dig the bog area, which in this project is a 4-ft.-dia. × 3-ft.-deep pit with straight sides. You can create a bog/pond filtration system on level ground, but if you're building on a slope, put the bog at the higher elevation to allow for a waterfall effect in the stream. Mound and tamp some of the excavated soil around the edges of the bog to create a berm for blocking runoff of lawn chemicals and grass clippings. In the floor of the bog, create a trench for the second culvert. Check that the culvert assemblies fit in the trenches of both the pond and the bog and adjust the soil as necessary. At the top of the stream, dig a deeper recess to act as a holding pond. Form the stream with stepped tiers, each with a gentle backward slope so that all of the water doesn't drain to the pond if the pump is turned off. The stream tiers must be level side to side. At the front edge of each step, form the grade level to be at least 6" higher than the stream. Finally, dig a narrow 12"-deep trench (sloping slightly towards the pump) next to the water feature. This is where you will bury the flexible PVC tubing that carries the water from the pump to the bog.

✎ UNDERLAYMENT AND LINER

Polyethylene fabric underlayment (similar to felt) protects the waterproof liner from rough surfaces as it is compressed under tons of rocks and water. The underlayment may be installed in overlapping pieces. (Do not substitute newspaper or old carpet.) The waterproof liner, a 45-mil EPDM rubber material made for ponds, is resistant to damage from temperature extremes, UV rays, and ice, and it is safe for fish and plants. (Rubber roofing material is not recommended.) We used flexible pond liner from Beckett (see Resources on page 234). Pond liner comes in various lengths and widths so you can line most water features with a single sheet. If you build an extra-large water feature, you'll need to seam the sections of liner according to the manufacturer's instructions. To calculate the size liner you need, add 2 times the pond depth plus the pond's maximum width plus 2 feet (for 1 foot of overhang on each side). Repeat for the entire length of the water feature.

EPDM liner

Underlayment

(continued)

Install the underlayment in sections, overlapping them so there are no gaps of exposed ground. Remember to avoid foot traffic near the edges of the excavation. Before placing the underlayment, clear away all sticks, roots, stones, etc.

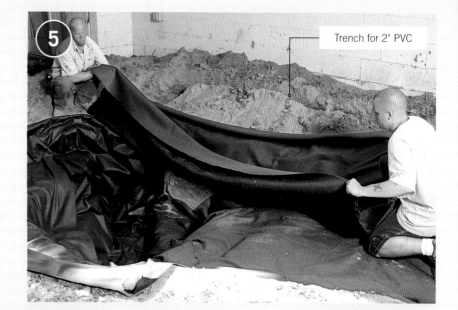

Trench for 2" PVC

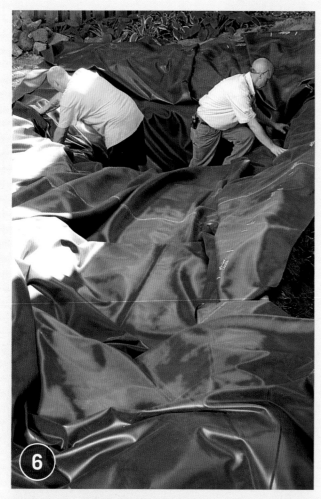

The liner is flexible but bulky, so enlist help if possible. Begin at the pond end, allowing 1 ft. of excess to drape over the edges. Expect some folds and wrinkles, but press the liner snugly into the tiers and corners. As you install the waterproof liner, be sure to press the liner tightly into curves and corners so the weight of rocks and water will not stretch it across any voids. Arrange the liner so at least 1 ft. wraps over the edges of the entire water feature.

Prepare the culvert pipe for installation. First, cut a section to fit the full length of the pond and a second piece that matches the depth of the pond when the sections are attached to the elbow. With a 2" hole saw, bore two rows of holes in the culvert to within 1 ft. of each end. Drill around ten holes in each section of culvert for the pond bed and bog bed, but none in the vertical sections.

Assemble the main culvert line to the vertical culvert type with the elbow fitting as a connector. Fasten coupler (or sleeve) straps around the joint between the culvert tubing and elbow and then lace the ends together with zip straps.

Install the culvert assembly in the trenches of the pond and bog, making sure the tops of the vertical sections are about 2" below grade at both ends of the system. The pond's horizontal culvert should slope slightly toward the elbow. Surround both culvert assemblies with large rocks to secure them. Trim the underlayment and EPDM liner to 1 ft. along the edges of the water feature. You can trim them to 6" after the water feature is lined with rock and filled with water.

Attach the PVC tube to the pump by twisting the male/female connector onto the threaded outlet of the pump. Apply PVC primer and glue to the 2" tubing and twist to evenly distribute the adhesive as you insert it into the threaded connector. Hold the assembly until the adhesive cures.

(continued)

Once the joint is set, lower the pump into the vertical culvert tube in the pond area.

After lowering the pump into the culvert, cut the PVC and install a 2" hose clamp to create a joint that enables you to disconnect the line if you need to replace or remove the pump.

Hose clamp

Ball valve

Trench

Ball valve

Bog

Cut the PVC tube again, at grade level, and rejoin it with a 2" ball shutoff valve in case you need to stop the flow of water when the pump is not on. Lay the tubing in the narrow trench next to the water feature so it extends from the pump to the floor of the bog. Install a second ball valve just above grade at the bog end as well. Then insert the tube into the horizontal end of the bog culvert.

STOCKING YOUR POND

Before choosing water-garden plants, talk with experts to learn which plants are hardy in your area. You'll want to eventually cover at least one-third of the pond surface with a variety of plants, including water lilies, marginals (shallow-water plants, such as iris and grasses), and oxygenators (such as water hyacinth). You can plant grasses in the bog area as well, which will eventually spread to cover the gravel bed of the bog.

Planting is easy. Just remove the plant from the pot, wash all of the soil from the roots and bury the roots directly in the gravel. Start with hardy perennials and gradually add tropical plants if you desire.

Once the water and plants are in place, complete the ecosystem by adding fish. Start with young koi (or goldfish) so they learn about the dangers of predators in a natural setting. When adding to an existing fish population, quarantine newcomers in a separate tank for a couple of weeks to ensure they are healthy. Follow the supplier's advice on how to acclimate fish to a new body of water. Although fish require initial care, don't be intimidated; you may soon find that they are your favorite part of being master of your own ecosystem.

Begin to add the boulders and rocks. To avoid foot traffic on the liner, stand in the hole and have someone hand you the rocks so you can position them. Starting with the largest rocks, fill around the culvert assembly in the pond. Add smaller rocks as you go, filling spaces between the larger ones. Periodically check that the liner fits against the soil as tightly as possible and that it reaches well over the edges of the excavated area. Adjust folds to distribute them evenly and minimize bulk.

Work your way upstream, setting large rocks along the sides and in front of the stepped edges. Line the bog with rock as described for the pond, starting with the largest rocks and fitting smaller ones between. Fill to about two-thirds full; then add gravel (1½"- to 2"-dia. river rock) to fill nearly to the top of the bog. Layer at least 3" of additional gravel on the floors of the pond and stream to create a bed for plants and to hide the liner. Build from the pond toward the bog with the largest rocks around the perimeter and along tiers to create rock walls in the pond and on the front of each tier in the stream. Cover the top of each culvert assembly with flagstone and a few decorative rocks. Place more rocks of varying sizes and colors around the entire water feature, in random positions for a natural look. Backfill the trench that holds the 2" flexible PVC tube.

Apply waterfall foam sealant to form a dam behind and under the ledge rocks in the stream so water is forced to flow over rather than under them.

Pack gravel to fill voids between the large and medium rocks to help secure them and all around the perimeter of the water feature to create a more natural look.

With the components in place, it's time to add water, plants, and fish. As you fill the water feature, rinse dirt off of the rocks and gravel. The water will be muddy at first—and after significant rains—but it will clear up within a few days.

Entertainment Projects for Landscapes

What's the point of creating a beautifully landscaped backyard if you don't use and enjoy it? This final chapter contains a few projects that are designed to equip your yard for backyard entertaining.

For pizza lovers, here's something to chew on: with the help of this chapter, the quest for the best pizza joint in town will end in your own backyard.

Really? Build a custom outdoor oven so you can create a fantastic wood-fired pizza whenever you hear the call of hand-tossed crust covered with pepperoni? That project has to be too complicated, you may think.

Nope. In this chapter, you'll find a prefabricated dome and a simplified-but-rustic-looking base that combine to make construction doable.

In addition, two other projects will make your backyard a neighborhood hot spot. One is an outdoor fireplace that includes a chimney and a hearth. No previous masonry experience is required. The same for our backyard fire pit, which is constructed around a metal liner and serves as a focal point and gathering spot.

The final project is not so hot—but it's way cool. It's an arbor retreat that provides an airy, sun-filtered space to sit on shaded benches and stay comfortable on glorious summer days. We have twenty-one step-by-step photos showing you how to build this beauty.

No matter which project you choose, you're going to want to stay a while—especially for the pizza.

In This Chapter:
- Backyard Fireplace
- Backyard Fire Pit
- Outdoor Brick Oven
- Arbor Retreat

Backyard Fireplace

For a backyard escape or a front-yard social spark, a wood-burning fireplace can't be beat. Sure, a fire pit may cost less and be easier to build, but an open-burning campfire can't hold a candle to a fireplace when it comes to comfort, safety, and stature. The chimney directs smoke up and away from onlookers; the hearth corrals flames, sparks, and ashes; and the stone-covered structure provides an attractive focal point for your landscape.

If you've lived with a smoky, inefficient fireplace, you know that good design is essential to the structure's performance. Therefore, building a brick-and-mortar fireplace is best left to professionals. But precast kits that are precisely shaped and sized to promote proper burning and ventilation can make constructing an outdoor fireplace almost as easy as stacking building blocks and frosting a layer cake. It requires a little more muscle and sweat, but the results will be smokin'.

TOOLS & MATERIALS

Compactable gravel	Wheelbarrow
Sand	Mortar-mixing hoe
Concrete mix	Rubber mallet
Rebar and metal mesh	and hammer
6 to 8 bricks or flat stones	Levels (three to four
6-mil poly sheeting	various sizes)
2 × 6 lumber	Concrete trowel
Concrete blocks (CMUs)	Hawk and trowel
Fireplace concrete units	Small hand grinder or
Adhesive mortar	masonry saw equipped
Stone veneer, brick	with a diamond blade
or stucco	Mason's trowel
Type N mortar	Margin trowel
Safety glasses, hearing	Large nippers or hatchet
protection, dust	Grout bag
mask, heavy gloves,	Brick jointer
kneepads	Whisk broom

To make this fire feature, plan on working for portions of three weekends: one to form the base, another to assemble the components, and a third to apply the stone or stucco veneer. Order the materials and gather tools and equipment ahead of time, and be sure to round up some help: Pouring the slab and assembling the fireplace require two people (preferably brawny ones).

Whether you live on a city lot or a country estate, check ordinances related to recreational fires and placement of a fireplace structure. Local code requirements may drive location decisions and will define any rules of operation for an outdoor fireplace. Of course, consider convenience and aesthetics as well as orientation with the landscape and the direction of prevailing winds, which could affect how smoke draws.

With this preformed, kit-style system, an outdoor fireplace is a great "D-I-Why-not?" project. No previous masonry experience is required.

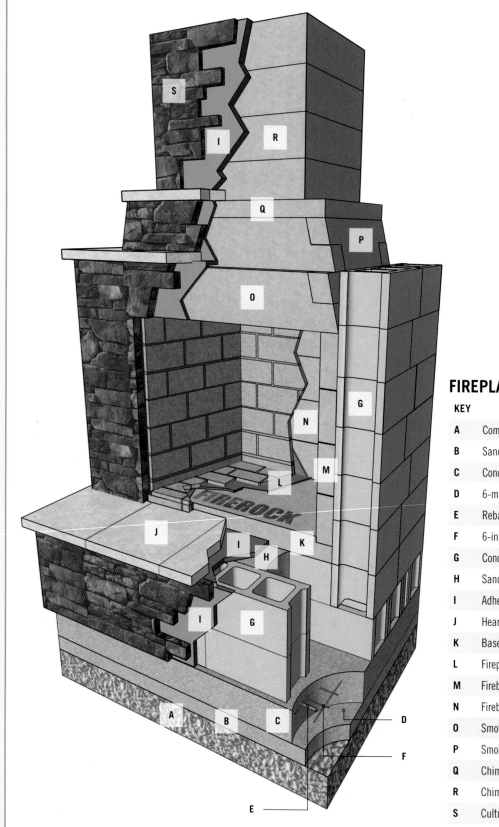

FIREPLACE PARTS

KEY

A	Compactable gravel
B	Sand
C	Concrete
D	6-mil plastic sheeting
E	Rebar
F	6-in. OC wire mesh
G	Concrete masonry units (CMUs)
H	Sand to fill large voids
I	Adhesive mortar
J	Hearthstone
K	Base plate
L	Fireproof mortar
M	Firebox side block
N	Firebox back block
O	Smoke chamber front
P	Smoke chamber side
Q	Chimney base
R	Chimney block
S	Cultured stone

BUILD A CONCRETE FIREPLACE PAD

Creating a concrete slab is simple, but the labor is not easy. Here are the DIY steps—which are best done not by yourself, but with helper.

Mark the dimensions of the fireplace base plus any hearth and side extensions. Remove 9 inches of soil and fill the area with 6 inches of compacted gravel, tamping after each 2 inches layer. Top with a 3 inches layer of sand and 6-mil plastic sheeting.

Build a frame of 2 × 6 lumber, ensuring that it is square, and place it over the area. Drive stakes around the outside perimeter to keep the frame from bowing outward with the weight of the concrete. Check that all of the tops are level. To maintain the frame's position, tack it to the stakes. Place bricks or 3-inch-diameter stones within the area to support three strips of rebar and mesh (leaving about 2 inches of space between the frame and the rebar or mesh).

Mix concrete (we used twelve 80-pound bags of concrete mix), following the directions on the bag. Pour to fill the boxed area, being careful not to disturb the structural metal. Use a flat trowel to smooth the surface and screed the top using a straight-edged board spanning the frame. To ensure proper curing, prevent the concrete from drying too quickly by periodically misting water on the surface and covering it with plastic. The setting time will depend on the concrete mixture and the humidity and temperature.

Make a 2 × 6 form staked over a sub-base of compacted gravel. Add pieces of No. 3 rebar for reinforcement. Fill the form with concrete.

Strike off the concrete then smooth it with a concrete trowel once the bleed water has evaporated.

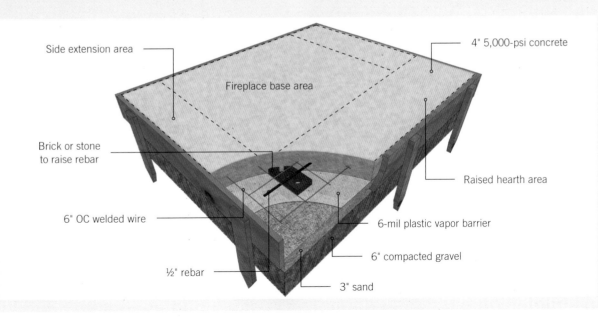

Side extension area

4" 5,000-psi concrete

Fireplace base area

Brick or stone to raise rebar

Raised hearth area

6" OC welded wire

6-mil plastic vapor barrier

6" compacted gravel

½" rebar

3" sand

How to Build a Backyard Fireplace

①

②

Once the concrete pad is dried (see previous page), begin stacking the concrete masonry units (CMUs) for the support base according to the plan. Take some time to first dry-assemble the components (as a "dress rehearsal") to prevent delays once you're applying mortar. In most cases, you'll need to cut some of the CMUs to fit. An angle grinder with a diamond blade is a good tool for this job. Disassemble the dry-fit blocks, keeping track of which block goes where.

Assemble the core structure from the CMUs, using heat-resistant mortar to bond the units together. Refer to information on building with concrete block if you are unsure how to accomplish this. Apply adhesive mortar to the joints between and under the CMUs. Check often to ensure that the tops are level and sides are plumb; pound high spots with a mallet and add mortar to areas that are low. To block air movement, fill the voids between the ends of the CMUs with mortar.

Base plate

Bead of mortar

③

④

Apply a heavy bed of mortar to the block foundation just inside the perimeter of the space for the base plate (a precast, prestressed slab that comes with the fireplace kit). A mortar bag—similar to a pastry bag—works best for this job. Carefully set the base on top of the mortar and foundation.

Level the fireplace base. It's vital that this unit be level side to side and front to back. Use the mallet and/or additional mortar, as needed, to make adjustments. Scrape off excess mortar that oozes out of joints.

To build the firebox, set the first tier of the sides and back, following the above procedure of applying a generous amount of mortar and adjusting for level in both directions. Continue with the next three tiers.

Once the four tiers of the firebox are complete, you're ready to add the eight smoke-chamber components. Set the front, the back and then the sides, filling all joints with mortar and checking for level with each addition. Repeat for the second course.

After adding the chimney base, install six courses of CMUs on each side of the firebox to add width to the fireplace. This step is optional, depending on the design and scale of the look you want to achieve.

Four chimney blocks complete the construction of the fireplace core. Because this is an outdoor fireplace, a damper is not needed for controlling the flow of air. Always refer to the kit manufacturer's instructions for more construction details and for safe operation recommendations.

(continued)

Install the corner stones, leaving ½" spaces above and below for mortar joints. Using a trowel, spread a ½"-thick layer of Type N mortar on the rear surface of a stone and jiggle the stone as you press it onto the surface. Scrape away the mortar that oozes out along the edges.

To achieve a finished firebox interior, cover the floor, sides and back with veneer firebrick (which is heat-tempered to withstand direct contact with fire). Be sure to use mortar and grout that can withstand high temperatures.

Add pieces to fill in the front and side faces, trimming stones as needed with large nippers or a mason's hammer. Again, generously "butter" the backs with mortar and leave ½" grout joints at the ends. Keep the concrete substrate slightly damp by misting it occasionally with a garden sprayer or hose.

Using a grout bag, carefully squeeze at least a ½"-thick bead of mortar between the stones. Avoid spilling too much on the stone surfaces around the joints—it's hard to get off.

Use a brick jointer or wooden dowel to press and smooth the grout lines. Do not get too aggressive here and displace the grout.

When the mortar is slightly dry, clean the stones' surfaces with a stiff-bristled broom. Avoid wiping with your hand or a cloth as it can smear the mortar into the stone. Then, brush between the stones to create a natural and consistent texture in the grout lines.

For a custom fit, cut the hearth and ledge stones using a power masonry saw equipped with a diamond blade.

Apply a generous amount of adhesive mortar to set the hearth and ledge stones. Check and adjust for level in both directions, pounding high areas with a mallet and adding mortar under the low spots.

OUTDOOR FIREPLACE SAFETY

Whenever you're operating a fireplace, safety is paramount. Always take these precautions:

- Keep water or a fire extinguisher nearby.

- Make sure any combustibles are a safe distance from the fireplace.

- Do not leave the fire unattended.

- Carefully monitor pets and kids.

- Burn only clean fuels (no trash, leaves, etc.).

- Be sure to extinguish the fire completely before you leave.

- Dispose of ashes only after you are certain they are cold.

One more rule: Fires are more fun when they're surrounded by friends and family. So invite your loved ones to celebrate your latest addition with a fireplace-warming party.

Backyard Fire Pit

A fire pit is a backyard focal point and gathering spot. The one featured here is constructed around a metal liner, which will keep the fire pit walls from overheating and cracking if cooled suddenly by rain or a bucket of water. The liner here is a section of 36-inch-diameter corrugated culvert pipe. Check local codes for stipulations on pit area size. Many codes require a 20-foot-diameter pit area.

Ashlar wall stones add character to the fire pit walls, but you can use any type of stone, including cast concrete retaining wall blocks. You'll want to prep the base for the seating area as you dig the fire pit to be sure both rest on the same level plane.

TOOLS & MATERIALS

Wheelbarrow
Landscape paint
String and stakes
Spades
Metal pipe
Landscape edging
Level
Garden rake
Plate vibrator
Metal firepit liner
Compactable gravel
Topdressing rock (trap rock)
Wall stones
Eye protection and work gloves

Some pointers to consider when using your fire pit include: 1) Make sure there are no bans or restrictions in effect; 2) Evaluate wind conditions and avoid building a fire if winds are heavy and/or blowing toward your home; 3) Keep shovels, sand, water, and a fire extinguisher nearby; 4) Extinguish fire with water and never leave the fire pit unattended.

Cross-Section: Fire Pit

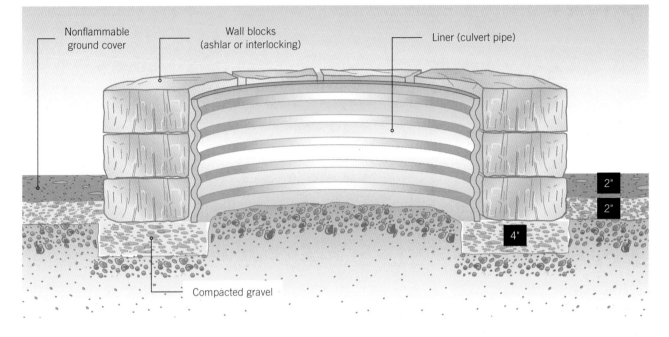

Nonflammable
ground cover

Wall blocks
(ashlar or interlocking)

Liner (culvert pipe)

2"

2"

4"

Compacted gravel

Plan View: Fire Pit

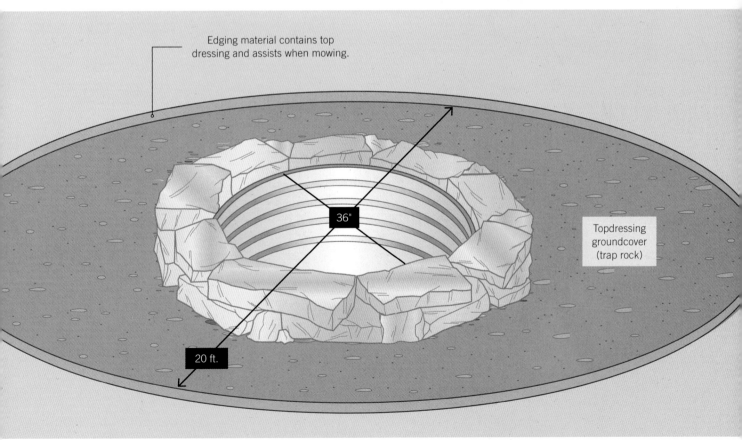

Edging material contains top
dressing and assists when mowing.

36"

20 ft.

Topdressing
groundcover
(trap rock)

How to Build a Fire Pit

Outline the location for your fire pit and the fire pit safety area by drawing concentric circles with landscape paint using a string and pole for guidance.

10 ft. radius

Remove a 4"-deep layer of sod and dirt in the fire pit and safety areas (the depth of the excavation depends on what materials you're installing in the safety zone).

Dig a 4"-deep trench for the perimeter stones that will ring the pit liner.

Fill the trench for the perimeter stones with compactable gravel and tamp thoroughly. Then scatter gravel to within 2½" of the paver edging top throughout the project area. It is not necessary to tamp this layer at this time.

Place your metal fire ring so it is level on the gravel layer and centered around the center pipe.

Arrange the first course of wall blocks around the fire ring. Keep gaps even and check with a level, adding or removing gravel as needed.

Install the second course of retaining wall block, taking care to evenly stagger the vertical joints on the first and second courses. Add the remaining courses.

Compact the compactable gravel in the seating/safety area using a rental plate vibrator.

Place and compact a layer of topdressing rock in the seating/safety area to complete the fire pit.

Outdoor Brick Oven

A good wood-fired pizza can make anyone dream of owning a custom outdoor oven. If you think such a project is too complicated for you to build, think again. Today's complete building kits simplify construction and still create that sought-after rustic look and incomparable flavor. Here you'll find details about a few different construction options as well as simple step-by-step plans for the project shown in the photos.

Using a prefabricated oven dome takes much of the intimidation out of the equation. The cooking technology is figured out for you and contained in a modular piece, making the project much easier and freeing you to focus on customizing the structure.

This project features low-dome construction that pulls the flame horizontally across the top of the oven and then vertically down the side, helping to produce higher temperatures for better cooking. The versatile unit also allows for three different types of cooking (radiant heat, convection, and conduction), making it versatile and a true kitchen fixture.

The unit comes with a dome, a hearth, an arch, some insulation materials, and a few other necessities and accessories. The rest of the structure shown here consists of a supportive base with space for wood storage and an oven surround with a chimney.

The only pizza better than pizzeria-style wood-fired pizza is wood-fired pizza made in your own backyard.

TOOLS & MATERIALS

Concrete mix (enough to fill the 5 × 5-ft. foundation and footings)

Wall stone: 4 × 8 × 12 in. (118); 4 × 8 × 8 in. (12); 4 × 4 × 8 in. (136—includes four extras for cutting around the oven arch); 4 × 4 × 12 in. (12)

Bluestone: 1 × 18 × 24 in. (1); ½ × 18 × 18 in. (1)

Indiana limestone slabs: 2 × 17 × 64 in. (12); 2 × 13 × 54 in. (4); 2 × 18 × 18 in. (1)

Over unit (Chicago Brick Oven model 750- See Resources, page 234)

Chimney pipe and cap compatible with the oven's anchor plate

How to Build an Outdoor Brick Oven

Create a sturdy foundation. First build a 5 × 5-ft. frame using 2 × 6 boards. Then dig around the frame 6" deep in the location where you plan to place the oven. Level the frame carefully, as the top of it will be the top of your finished concrete foundation. Next, dig four holes at the corners for footings. Add rebar inside the footing holes and within the frame for stability.

Fill the footing holes and the frame with concrete; then use a screed to level the top so that it is flush with the top of the frame. Let the concrete cure for two days.

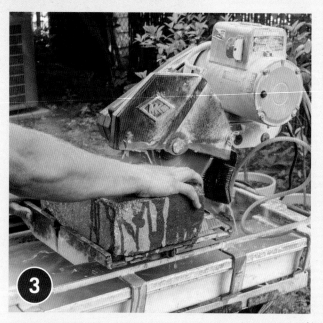

Using a wet tile saw, cut the wall stones for the first two courses according to the materials list. For this project as shown, you'll need to cut several wall stones to size. A wet tile saw is a handy tool to have for the task, as it cuts quickly and minimizes dust. If you don't own a heavy-duty wet tile saw, consider renting one for a day or two.

Lay the first two courses of stone blocks. Draw a line to mark the center of the front and back of the concrete pad; then, place the first stone so that it is centered on the line. Continue laying out the first course of stones, making sure that all four sides of the course are square. Stack the second course on top of the first. No mortar was used in the oven base.

Next, place limestone slabs (four 17" × 64" slabs of Indiana limestone are shown here) on top of the second course of wall stones. This forms the base for the wood-storage space. Cut and lay the next four courses of wall stones and slabs. Two more courses of wall stones and four more limestone slabs come next.

Add the oven dome. The unit seen here comes with three insulation boards that must be placed under the dome. Enlist the help of a few friends and lower the oven dome into position. It is extremely heavy and requires precise placement on the insulation boards on the base of the structure. It's beneficial to use scraps of cardboard under the oven dome as you maneuver it to prevent scratching the limestone slab. Attach the chimney anchor box, wrap the dome with the insulation blanket and then attach the oven arch and door.

The second layer of four 2" × 17" × 64" Indiana limestone slabs tops off the base of the backyard oven structure. As shown in the photo, the open space created by the previous four courses of wall stones is perfect for storing plenty of firewood. Once the base structure is complete, you're ready to move on to building the oven-surround structure.

TEXTURE THE SLAB EDGES

You can save some money by rock-facing the edges of the limestone slabs yourself using a carbide-tip chisel and bell hammer. This will give you the rough, rustic-looking edges shown in the photos.

(continued)

Cut the next five courses of wall stones to size. With the oven dome centered on the base of the structure, lay out the first course of wall stones for the surround according to the illustrations. Make sure all sides are square.

Secure each course of the surround structure in place using high-heat-rated construction adhesive. Check each course as you go to make sure that the surround structure remains level and square.

This photo shows what the oven surround will look like once all five courses of wall stones are in place. Use composite shims where needed to keep each course level. Cut off the overhanging pieces of the shims and clean up adhesive squeezeout after the adhesive has cured. Note that the placement of the oven and surround on the base structure creates a useful countertop space.

Add the four 2 × 13 × 54-in. limestone roof pieces; cut a hole for the chimney pipe to pass through. Add heat-resistant mortar between these pieces to prevent water from entering the oven surround.

Add a decorative touch by cutting pieces of ½"-thick bluestone to fit around the oven arch (inset photo). Mark the size, number, and location of bluestone pieces around the oven arch using a carpenter's pencil. Note that these pieces will overlap some of the surround wall stones as well as the oven arch.

OPTION: Cut out spaces for the door hardware, which helps to add a hand-crafted touch.

Finish by sealing any gaps in the roof and around the base of the surround with high-heat-rated clear silicone caulk. This includes the chimney and surrounding wall stones, around the chimney cap, along the base of the surround, etc. Most backyard ovens must be cured before they are ready to start cooking. Burn a few low-heat fires (212° F or less) over the course of a few days to slowly release all moisture. Then you're ready to start cooking!

Stack three courses of wall stones around the chimney pipe. Then add the final limestone cap, cut to fit around the chimney pipe.

TIP: Cut the chimney cap into two pieces. Add heat-resistant mortar to all seams in the limestone cap.

Arbor Retreat

The airy, sun-filtered space under an arbor always makes you want to stay awhile—thus, it's a perfect place for built-in seating. The arbor getaway we've chosen (facing page) has plenty of room for lounging or visiting, but it's designed to do much more: viewed from the front, the arbor retreat becomes an elegant passageway. The bench seating is obscured by latticework, and your eyes are drawn toward the central opening and striking horizontal beams. This makes the structure perfect as a grand garden entrance or a landscape focal point. For added seclusion, tuck this arbor behind some foliage.

Sitting inside the retreat you can enjoy privacy and shade behind the lattice screens. The side roof sections over the seats are lowered to follow a more human scale and create a cozier sense of enclosure. Each bench comfortably fits three people and the two sides face each other at a range that's ideal for conversation.

A classic archway with a keystone motif gives this arbor retreat its timeless appeal.

An arbor with benches makes an ideal resting spot that will become a destination when hiking to remote areas of your property.

A slatted roof and lattice walls are designed to cut sun and wind, creating a comfortable environment inside the arbor retreat.

A few subtle touches turn this cedar arbor into a true standout. The arches at the tops of the sidewall panels give the design visual lift and a touch of Oriental styling.

ARBOR RETREAT

MATERIALS LIST

DESCRIPTION (NO. FINISHED PIECES)	QUANTITY/SIZE	MATERIAL
POSTS		
Inner posts (4)	4 @ field measure	4 × 4
Outer posts (4)	4 @ field measure	4 × 4
Concrete	Field measure	3,000 PSI concrete
Gravel	Field measure	Compactable gravel
ROOF		
Beams (6 main, 4 cross)	8 @ 8'	4 × 4
Roof slats (10 lower, 11 upper)	21 @ 8'	2 × 2
SEATS		
Seat supports, spacers, slats (6 horizontal supports, 6 vertical supports, 4 spacers, 16 slats)	16 @ 8'	2 × 6
Aprons (2)	2 @ 6'	1 × 8
LATTICE SCREENS		
Arches (4)	1 @ 8'	2 × 8
Slats—arched sides (20 horizontal, 8 vertical)	12 @ 8'	2 × 2
Slats—back (8)	8 @ 8'	2 × 2
HARDWARE & FASTENERS		
⅜" × 7" galvanized lag screws	12, with washers	
3" deck screws		
3½" deck screws		
2½" deck screws		
¼" × 3" galvanized lag screws	16, with washers	

FRONT ELEVATION

BEAM END DETAIL

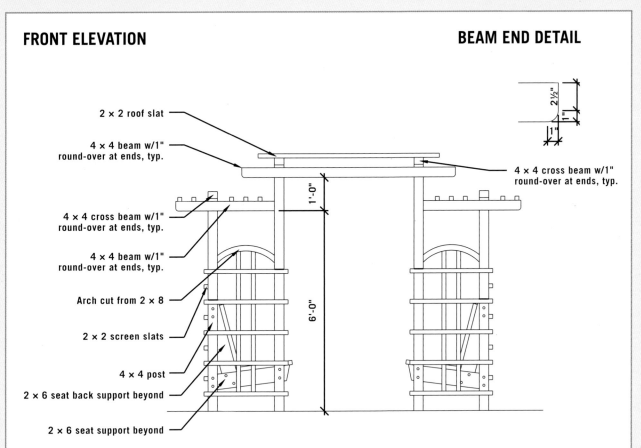

2 × 2 roof slat

4 × 4 beam w/1" round-over at ends, typ.

4 × 4 cross beam w/1" round-over at ends, typ.

4 × 4 beam w/1" round-over at ends, typ.

Arch cut from 2 × 8

2 × 2 screen slats

4 × 4 post

2 × 6 seat back support beyond

2 × 6 seat support beyond

4 × 4 cross beam w/1" round-over at ends, typ.

2½"

1"

1"

1'-0"

6'-0"

SIDE ELEVATION

POST LAYOUT

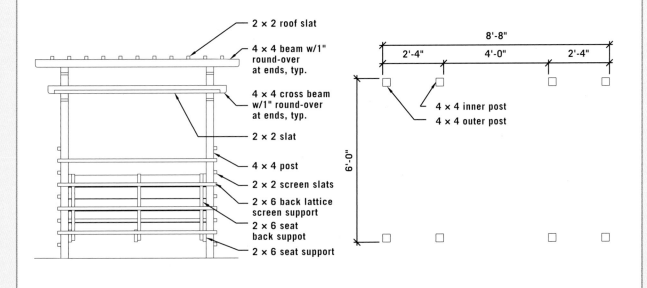

2 × 2 roof slat

4 × 4 beam w/1" round-over at ends, typ.

4 × 4 cross beam w/1" round-over at ends, typ.

2 × 2 slat

4 × 4 post

2 × 2 screen slats

2 × 6 back lattice screen support

2 × 6 seat back suppot

2 × 6 seat support

8'-8"

2'-4"   4'-0"   2'-4"

4 × 4 inner post

4 × 4 outer post

6'-0"

UPPER LEVEL ROOF FRAMING PLAN

SEAT FRAMING PLAN

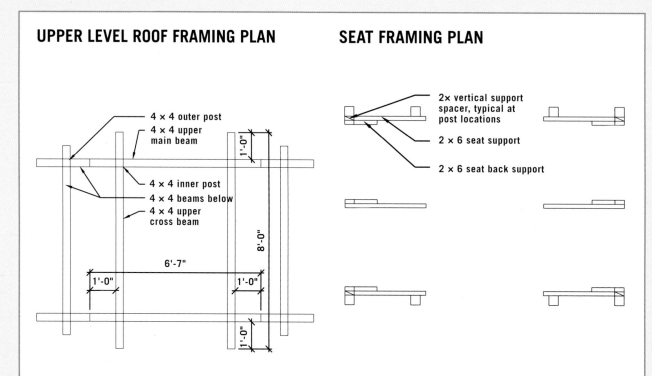

4 × 4 outer post

4 × 4 upper main beam

4 × 4 inner post

4 × 4 beams below

4 × 4 upper cross beam

1'-0"

8'-0"

6'-7"

1'-0"

1'-0"

1'-0"

2× vertical support spacer, typical at post locations

2 × 6 seat support

2 × 6 seat back support

ROOF/SLAT PLAN

SLAT PLAN @ SEATING

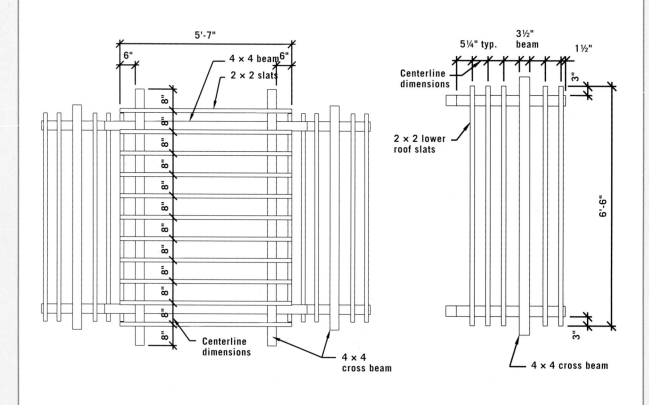

5'-7"

6"

4 × 4 beam

6"

2 × 2 slats

8"
8"
8"
8"
8"
8"
8"
8"
8"
8"
8"

Centerline dimensions

4 × 4 cross beam

5¼" typ.

3½" beam

1½"

3"

Centerline dimensions

2 × 2 lower roof slats

6'-6"

3"

4 × 4 cross beam

SEAT SECTION

ARCH DETAIL/SCREEN LAYOUT

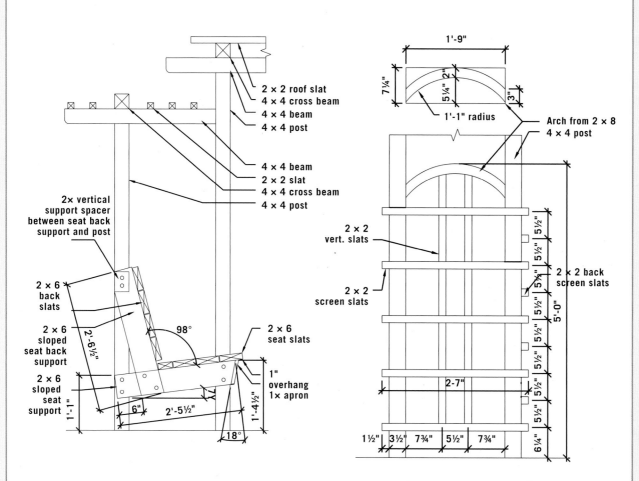

2 × 2 roof slat
4 × 4 cross beam
4 × 4 beam
4 × 4 post

4 × 4 beam
2 × 2 slat
4 × 4 cross beam
4 × 4 post

2× vertical support spacer between seat back support and post

2 × 6 back slats

2 × 6 sloped seat back support

2 × 6 sloped seat support

98°

2'-6½"

2 × 6 seat slats

1" overhang 1× apron

1'-1"

6" 2'-5½"

18°

1'-4½"

1'-9"

7¼" 5¼" 2" 3"

1'-1" radius

Arch from 2 × 8
4 × 4 post

2 × 2 vert. slats

2 × 2 screen slats

2 × 2 back screen slats

5'-0"

5½" 5½" 5½" 5½" 5½" 5½" 5½" 5½" 5½"

2-7"

1½" 3½" 7¾" 5½" 7¾"

6¼"

SEAT LEVEL ROOF FRAMING PLAN

SEAT SLAT LAYOUT PLAN

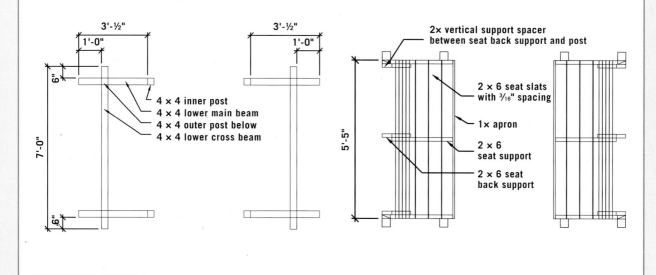

3'-½"
1'-0"
6"

7'-0"

6"

3'-½"
1'-0"

4 × 4 inner post
4 × 4 lower main beam
4 × 4 outer post below
4 × 4 lower cross beam

2× vertical support spacer between seat back support and post

5'-5"

2 × 6 seat slats with ³⁄₁₆" spacing

1× apron

2 × 6 seat support

2 × 6 seat back support

Stake out the project area. Drive a pair of stakes about 2 ft. outside of each corner and string mason's lines from the stakes to create a rectangle that's equal to the total project footprint (6 ft. × 8 ft. 8" as seen here). Mark post locations on the strings, as shown in the Post Layout diagram, and drive stakes at those points to mark postholes.

Trim post tops. Let the concrete set up overnight and then mark level cutting lines on the posts tops. Use a laser level or a 4 ft. level taped to a straight 2 × 4 to transfer the cutting lines. Make sure to make all four faces of each post. Use a circular saw (a cordless trim saw is best) to trim the post tops.

Set the eight posts in concrete, making sure that the tops of the four inner posts are at least 84" above the ground, and the four outer posts are 72" above ground. The size and depth of postholes should conform to local building codes. At a minimum, the postholes should be three times the diameter of the post (a 12"-dia. hole) and 24" deep. Use stakes and braces to level and plumb the posts.

Install the lower beams. For each lower level main beam, set the beam on top of an outer post and butt its unshaped end against the corresponding inner post. Hold the beam level and mark the point where the top face of the beam meets the inner post. Set the beam aside.

4

Cut the lower and upper level beams. The lower level consists of four beams running perpendicular to the seats and two beams running parallel to the seats. The upper level has two main beams and two cross beams. The 4 × 4 beams have two ends rounded over at the bottom corners with a jig saw. Cut the lower seat level beams to length at 36½". Cut the lower cross beams at 84". Cut upper level main beams to length at 79". Cut upper level cross beams at 96".

5

6

Mark a drilling point for a pilot hole on the opposite (inside) face of the inner post. Then, drill a counterbored hole just deep enough to completely recess the washer and head of a ⅜" × 7" lag screw. Reposition each beam so its top face is on the post reference line. Then drill a pilot hole for the lag screw through the inner post and into the end of the beam. Fasten each main beam with a ⅜" lag screw.

(continued)

Drill angled pilot holes through the sides of the cross beams and into the main beams, about ¾" in from the sides of the main beams (to avoid hitting the large screws). Drill two holes on each side of the cross beam at each joint. Fasten cross beams to main beams with 3½" deck screws (eight screws for each cross beam) driven toenail style.

Cut the ten lower roof slats to length (78"). Mark the roof slat layout onto the tops of the lower main beams, following the plan on page 224. Position slats so they overhang the main beams by 3" at both ends. Drill pilot holes, and fasten the slats to the main beams with 2½" deck screws.

Cut seat supports according to the Seat Framing Plan on page 224. Save the cutoffs to make seat slats. Also cut a pair of vertical support spacers from a full 2 × 6. Test-fit the pieces onto the arbor posts and make necessary adjustments. Make 18°-plumb cuts at the fronts of the seat supports.

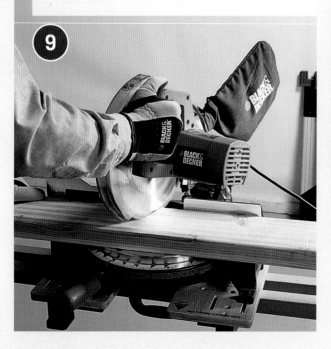

Position the horizontal seat supports by first measuring up from the ground and marking the inner posts at 16½" and the outer posts at 13". (This marks the top edges of the horizontal supports.) Next, position the seat supports on the marks so their back ends are flush with the outsides of the outer posts. Fasten the supports to the posts with ¼" × 3" lag screws driven through counterbored pilot holes.

Position the vertical seat back support spacers and mark the locations of the support spacer onto the post. Fasten spacers to the post with 3" deck screws driven through pilot holes. Then, fasten the vertical seat back support to the spacer and horizontal seat support with 3½" deck screws; use three or four screws at each end.

Measure and cut 1 × 8 aprons to lengths so they will fit between the outside faces of the side seat supports. Bevel-cut the top edges of the aprons at 7°. Position the aprons against the seat supports. Fasten aprons to the ends of seat supports with 3½" deck screws.

Install seat slats and center supports by first measuring between inner posts for seat slat length; then cutting eight slats for each side. Position a slat on top of the horizontal seat supports so the front edge overhangs the supports by about 1". Fasten the slat to supports with pairs of 3" deck screws. Continue installing slats, leaving a ³⁄₁₆" gap between each.

Assemble the two center seat supports so they match the outer supports, using 2½" deck screws. Install the center supports at the midpoints of the slats by screwing through the slats and into the supports, using 3" deck screws.

(continued)

Build arched lattice screens by first marking the layout of horizontal lattice pieces onto the posts. Mark along one post and use a level to transfer the marks to the other post. Then cut twenty 2 × 2 lattice slats to 31". Position them so they overhang the posts by 1½" at both ends and fasten slats to posts with 2½" deck screws driven through pilot holes.

Make the arches using a cardboard template to trace the shape onto a 2 × 8. Cut out the arch with a jigsaw or bandsaw and test-fit the arch between the post pairs. Make necessary adjustments and cut the remaining arches. Sand the cut edges smooth.

Fasten the arches to the posts using 2½" deck screws. First, position arches so they are flush with the outside faces of the posts and, at each end, drill an angled pilot hole upward through the bottom of the arch and into the post.

Cut eight vertical slats to a rough length of 54" (first, mark slats 7" from each post to represent the outside edges of the vertical lattice slats). Mark the top ends of the slats to match the arches by holding each slat on its reference marks. Cut the curved ends and test-fit the slats. Hold each slat in place against the arch (mark bottom for length), then cut them to length.

Install vertical slats with 3" deck screws driven down through tops of the arches and 2½" deck screws driven through the lowest horizontal slats. Make sure all screwheads are countersunk.

Build the back lattice screens by cutting 2 × 2 slats to length at 75", for a 1½" overhang at each end. Position the slats on layout marks, drill pilot holes, and fasten the slats to the posts with 2½" deck screws.

Finish the structure. Sand any rough areas with a random-orbit sander. Wipe down the project, and then apply a coat of exterior wood sealant/protectant.

Metric Conversions

ENGLISH TO METRIC

TO CONVERT:	TO:	MULTIPLY BY:
Inches	Millimeters	25.4
Inches	Centimeters	2.54
Feet	Meters	0.305
Yards	Meters	0.914
Square inches	Square centimeters	6.45
Square feet	Square meters	0.093
Square yards	Square meters	0.836
Ounces	Milliliters	30.0
Pints (U.S.)	Liters	0.473 (Imp. 0.568)
Quarts (U.S.)	Liters	0.946 (Imp. 1.136)
Gallons (U.S.)	Liters	3.785 (Imp. 4.546)
Ounces	Grams	28.4
Pounds	Kilograms	0.454

TO CONVERT:	TO:	MULTIPLY BY:
Millimeters	Inches	0.039
Centimeters	Inches	0.394
Meters	Feet	3.28
Meters	Yards	1.09
Square centimeters	Square inches	0.155
Square meters	Square feet	10.8
Square meters	Square yards	1.2
Milliliters	Ounces	.033
Liters	Pints (U.S.)	2.114 (Imp. 1.76)
Liters	Quarts (U.S.)	1.057 (Imp. 0.88)
Liters	Gallons (U.S.)	0.264 (Imp. 0.22)
Grams	Ounces	0.035
Kilograms	Pounds	2.2

CONVERTING TEMPERATURES

Convert degrees Fahrenheit (F) to degrees Celsius (C) by following this simple formula: Subtract 32 from the Fahrenheit temperature reading. Then multiply that number by $\frac{5}{9}$. For example, 77°F - 32 = 45. 45 × $\frac{5}{9}$ = 25°C.

To convert degrees Celsius to degrees Fahrenheit, multiply the Celsius temperature reading by $\frac{9}{5}$. Then, add 32. For example, 25°C × $\frac{9}{5}$ = 45. 45 + 32 = 77°F.

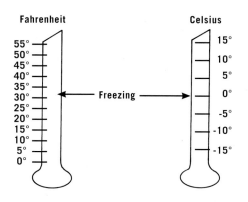

METRIC PLYWOOD PANELS

Metric plywood panels are commonly available in two sizes: 1,200 mm × 2,400 mm and 1,220 mm × 2,400 mm, which is roughly equivalent to a 4 × 8-ft. sheet. Standard and Select sheathing panels come in standard thicknesses, while Sanded grade panels are available in special thicknesses.

STANDARD SHEATHING GRADE		SANDED GRADE	
7.5 mm	($\frac{5}{16}$ in.)	6 mm	($\frac{4}{17}$ in.)
9.5 mm	($\frac{3}{8}$ in.)	8 mm	($\frac{5}{16}$ in.)
12.5 mm	($\frac{1}{2}$ in.)	11 mm	($\frac{7}{16}$ in.)
15.5 mm	($\frac{5}{8}$ in.)	14 mm	($\frac{9}{16}$ in.)
18.5 mm	($\frac{3}{4}$ in.)	17 mm	($\frac{2}{3}$ in.)
20.5 mm	($\frac{13}{16}$ in.)	19 mm	($\frac{3}{4}$ in.)
22.5 mm	($\frac{7}{8}$ in.)	21 mm	($\frac{13}{16}$ in.)
25.5 mm	(1 in.)	24 mm	($\frac{15}{16}$ in.)

LUMBER DIMENSIONS

NOMINAL - U.S.	ACTUAL - U.S. (IN INCHES)	METRIC
1 × 2	¾ × 1½	19 × 38 mm
1 × 3	¾ × 2½	19 × 64 mm
1 × 4	¾ × 3½	19 × 89 mm
1 × 5	¾ × 4½	19 × 114 mm
1 × 6	¾ × 5½	19 × 140 mm
1 × 7	¾ × 6¼	19 × 159 mm
1 × 8	¾ × 7¼	19 × 184 mm
1 × 10	¾ × 9¼	19 × 235 mm
1 × 12	¾ × 11¼	19 × 286 mm
1¼ × 4	1 × 3½	25 × 89 mm
1¼ × 6	1 × 5½	25 × 140 mm
1¼ × 8	1 × 7¼	25 × 184 mm
1¼ × 10	1 × 9¼	25 × 235 mm
1¼ × 12	1 × 11¼	25 × 286 mm
1½ × 4	1¼ × 3½	32 × 89 mm
1½ × 6	1¼ × 5½	32 × 140 mm
1½ × 8	1¼ × 7¼	32 × 184 mm
1½ × 10	1¼ × 9¼	32 × 235 mm
1½ × 12	1¼ × 11¼	32 × 286 mm
2 × 4	1½ × 3½	38 × 89 mm
2 × 6	1½ × 5½	38 × 140 mm
2 × 8	1½ × 7¼	38 × 184 mm
2 × 10	1½ × 9¼	38 × 235 mm
2 × 12	1½ × 11¼	38 × 286 mm
3 × 6	2½ × 5½	64 × 140 mm
4 × 4	3½ × 3½	89 × 89 mm
4 × 6	3½ × 5½	89 × 140 mm

LIQUID MEASUREMENT EQUIVALENTS

1 Pint	= 16 Fluid Ounces	= 2 Cups
1 Quart	= 32 Fluid Ounces	= 2 Pints
1 Gallon	= 128 Fluid Ounces	= 4 Quarts

COUNTERBORE, SHANK & PILOT HOLE DIAMETERS

SCREW SIZE	COUNTERBORE DIAMETER FOR SCREW HEAD (IN INCHES)	CLEARANCE HOLE FOR SCREW SHANK (IN INCHES)	PILOT HOLE DIAMETER	
			HARD WOOD (IN INCHES)	SOFT WOOD (IN INCHES)
#1	.146 (9/64)	5/64	3/64	1/32
#2	1/4	3/32	3/64	1/32
#3	1/4	7/64	1/16	3/64
#4	1/4	1/8	1/16	3/64
#5	1/4	1/8	5/64	1/16
#6	5/16	9/64	3/32	5/64
#7	5/16	5/32	3/32	5/64
#8	3/8	11/64	1/8	3/32
#9	3/8	11/64	1/8	3/32
#10	3/8	3/16	1/8	7/64
#11	1/2	3/16	5/32	9/64
#12	1/2	7/32	9/64	1/8

NAILS

Nail lengths are identified by numbers from 4 to 60 followed by the letter "d," which stands for "penny." For general framing and repair work, use common or box nails. Common nails are best suited to framing work where strength is important. Box nails are smaller in diameter than common nails, which makes them easier to drive and less likely to split wood. Use box nails for light work and thin materials. Most common and box nails have a cement or vinyl coating that improves their holding power.

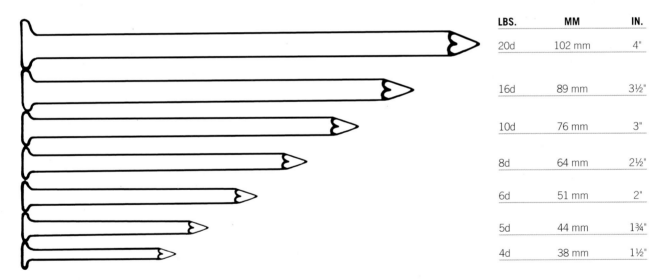

LBS.	MM	IN.
20d	102 mm	4"
16d	89 mm	3½"
10d	76 mm	3"
8d	64 mm	2½"
6d	51 mm	2"
5d	44 mm	1¾"
4d	38 mm	1½"

Resources

Belgard
Wall stones
877.235.4273
www.belgard.com

BLACK + DECKER™
Portable power tools and more
www.blackanddecker.com

Cali Bamboo
Bamboo fencing, flooring, and more
888.788.2254
www.calibamboo.com

California Redwood Association
www.calredwood.org

Call 811
Call before you dig
811
www.call811.com

Chicago Brick Oven
630.359.4793
www.chicagobrickoven.com

FireRock
888.876.1025
www.firerock.us

Mantels Direct
Outdoor fireplace mantels
855.849.2079
www.mantelsdirect.com

Precast Outdoor Fireplaces
508.378.7742
www.precastoutdoorfireplaces.com

Red Wing Shoes Co.
Work shoes and boots
800.733.9464
www.redwingshoes.com

Superior Clay Corp.
Fireplaces and chimney pots
800.848.6166
www.superiorclay.com

United States Department of Agriculture
USDA gardening zone maps
www.planthardiness.ars.usda.gov

Photo Credits

Architectural Landscape Design: 19 (top), 21 (top)

Astrid Gaiser Garden Design, LLC: 24

Belgard: 16

Borst Landscape and Design, Kathy King: 10, 26 (bottom)

Brian Vanden Brink: 25 (bottom)

Christensen Landscape Services: 27 (both)

iStock: 58, 67, 81, 186

Jerry Pavia: 96

Jessie Walker: 25 (top)

John Gregor/ColdSnap Photography: 3 (top), 23 (top)

John Rickard: 179 (bottom)

Luciole Design, Inc: 11 (top), 13 (top), 15 (both), 17 (top)

SCOUT: 5 (top, middle), 102, 103, 104, 105, 106, 107, 108, 176, 191, 192, 193 (bottom), 194, 195, 196, 197, 198, 199, 202, 203, 204, 205, 206, 207, 208, 209, 214, 215, 216, 217, 218, 219

Shelley Metcalf: 18 (top), 146

Shutterstock: 8, 12 (top left, bottom), 13 (bottom), 14 (bottom), 17 (bottom), 18 (bottom), 20 (both), 21 (bottom), 22 (both), 23 (bottom), 38, 40 (both), 41, 44 (both), 45 (both), 46 (top), 54, 66, 68, 70, 71 (all), 98 (both), 99 (bottom), 100 (all), 110, 132, 134, 178, 201

Index